T0248356

STAND ALONE

HOW TO BE AN EXTRAORDINARY LEADER

SABRINA LLOYD

SAVIO
REPVBLIC

A SAVIO REPUBLIC BOOK
An Imprint of Post Hill Press
ISBN: 978-1-63758-295-4
ISBN (eBook): 978-1-63758-296-1

posthillpress.com
New York • Nashville
Published in the United States of America

1 2 3 4 5 6 7 8 9 10

I would like to dedicate this work to who I dedicated my life to and who has always made me understand and know that I am never alone—God. And the greatest leader to ever live—Jesus.

"Men who have blazed new paths for civilization have always been precedent breakers. It is ever the man who is not afraid to STAND ALONE; who is bold, original, resourceful, that leaves his mark on his times."

—Orison Sweet Marden

CONTENTS

AUTHOR'S NOTE

I'VE ALWAYS BEEN an exceptional student. My natural curiosity for knowledge and ability to learn anything has allowed me to understand systems, people, and ideas. This has played a tremendous role in enriching my life overall. I hope to share all that I have learned with you to help you expand your own learnings and mind. After all, we see with our brains, not with our eyes. I'm going to help you see everything a little differently, so you can change and take charge of your life. You are not a victim of your life, your circumstances, or past. You are God's greatest creation, and everything He has given to you is an opportunity for you to reveal this to yourself.

My story is at the intersection of success in business and life, mixed with science and religion. I've been called everything from an angel to crazy. Both are true. This is the story of someone ordinary who became extraordinary because I gave it my all, which is exactly what you will learn when you take control of your life and Stand Alone.

No matter where you are in your journey, choose to be excellent at whatever you are doing. Excellence means you give your all. Only you can control your excellence—no one else has access to your power. One day, all the dots will connect for you, as they did for me and still are doing, even now. You will see that everything that is happening to you was actually designed for you in order to create a better version of you—if you will allow it.

INTRODUCTION

Y OU AND I are not the same now, but I once was you. I was that scared kid, insecure, frightened of my own shadow. If you've ever grown up in a house where there is violence, you know it changes you. Your innocence dies. You learn to read people differently. You learn to read situations differently. You study and become immersed in things that "normal" kids would never have to worry about.

You're a happy, free-spirited child one moment—and then the garage door opens. He's home. You pay attention to every sound differently. You scramble. Who's walking through the door today? Will it be a good day or will today be hell? It doesn't matter if you are a boy or a girl; something inside of you dies when you experience trauma in your own home.

Every child is born into this world innocent, and then life happens. Life is happening to all of us. When it's happening and you're in the midst of it all, it's important you see that everything is working to build a stronger version of you. It takes a very unique person to handle the worst challenges that can come your way and turn them into the best things that could have ever happened to you—because such difficulties have the power to shape you into who you were meant to be. When you can start to look at your life through the lens of everything working to build you and make you stronger, you can stop being a victim and start to separate yourself from the masses. This is when you realize your power—this is when you start to **Stand Alone**.

How does a scared little girl who is stripped of everything rebuild her life back stronger? When people see me today, they often think that I have everything. The truth is no one has everything. We are all struggling with something. How the outside world perceives us and how we perceive ourselves are two very different things, and how you think about yourself is the most important thing. I will never have everything I want because I'm constantly in pursuit of the greater version of myself, but at the same time, I feel whole. I am whole. We become whole when we look at life not in terms of what we are missing but what we have gained and are continuing to gain, including the most challenging times of our lives. Growth doesn't happen in good times. Growth happens in the moments of life that challenge and push us. These moments forge a new you. They chisel out your character by the decision you make to keep going and keep growing—or stop and disintegrate into victimhood. Everything that I experienced as a child and as an ambitious woman attempting to be the best wife, mother, and CEO have all made me who I am today. The truth is, if you were to take it all away from me, I'd still be OK because I've worked so hard to fully know myself. More than anything else, this has been an extraordinarily important goal of my life's work.

It hasn't been easy, but it's been worth it. Every hardship. Every disaster. Everything that I have suffered through and overcome. Every dark moment that I have experienced has allowed me to become the person who I am today. When I look back on my life, I realize now that my foundation was so important. Like a building being erected from the ground up—the strength of what that building can endure lies in its foundation. The taller the building, the deeper into the earth the foundations go. The materials that make the foundation have to be strong to withstand the normal wear and tear of nature.

Our foundation for our lives is how we were raised and what each experience that we ever go through means to us. How we interpret the wear and tear continues to either reinforce or strip away at our lives. This is true for every single one of us, and while hardship is extremely difficult to overcome, it's the exact thing that changes you and pushes you to become your best. It can set you up like no one else. If you've never had suffering or gone through difficulties, how can you push yourself to the limit? When you experience these things as a younger child, you are able to go through hardships later in life and business without being destroyed by them. For me, my most difficult moments became the moments that also transformed me into who I am today. Looking back, these are the exact things that pushed me to start leading my life instead of just letting things happen to me. You can do it, too.

DECIDING TO GO ALL IN

Whatever you're doing, you absolutely must decide to go all in. And I am here to tell you that no matter what you have been through, you can make the decision to walk towards the light. Like a broken bone, I had to grow back stronger and choose to become more resilient. The scars I have only mean that those people don't affect me anymore—they can't get to me now. These scars allow me to stand alone. They allow me to finally be free. This book is about unlocking something *deep* that lives inside of all of us. Very few will have the pain tolerance to tap into this side of themselves. It's a side of no-nonsense, no excuses, and a sick and twisted love and appreciation for pain and hardship because of what it will make of you.

When you ask God for something, He will never give you that exact thing directly. He will instead give you the opportunity to become the kind of man or woman who can have the thing that you so deeply desire. If you ask for a chair, he will direct you to a tree. But then it's you who has to take action. You need to start chopping and making the chair out of the raw materials that have been given to you. The same is true for leveling up your life and career. If you are asking for an extraordinary life, you better know that hell is coming for you. This is where the work begins, and this is the moment when you have to dig deeper to figure out what really matters to you.

Hell isn't the same for all of us. Some of us go through unimaginable things that would make someone else's hell look like a walk through the park. However true, I also believe that we're not given more than we're capable of handling. The hardships that I experienced could have been too much for someone else, but they were enough for me to push myself to another level of greatness. Everyone's hardships are their own, and they are all difficult and challenging. One does not diminish the other, though it's more about what you do with them. Whether our difficulties are small or large, when we are in our own hell and being asked to walk through it, the feeling of hardship we endure is all the same. It sucks. It's horrible, and all we want to do is simply find our way out. However true, going through it and getting to the other side is what you have to do in order to get to the real version of all that you can become. That's how you go from being someone ordinary to someone extraordinary.

> *"One has to investigate the principle in one thing or one event exhaustively.... Things and the self are governed by the same principle. If you understand one, you understand the other, for the truth within and the truth without are identical."*

> —*Er Cheng yishu, 11th century*

In my life, I have been forced to walk to the edge and bring myself back. I conquered so many difficulties and was able to rise above what life threw my way. And now that I've made it to the other side, I am willing to tell you what it really takes to create your own life instead of just living life by default. So many people are ill-equipped today to handle the hardships. Most people are either overly sensitive or simply anesthetized and, as such, detached from reality. All that is easily seen are the rewards and the outcomes because the only things people are willing to talk about are their great experiences and opportunities. We live in a world that's censored from reality—we only see the highlight reels and the good moments. We don't see the work and the hardships that went into getting there. I assure you there is a lot more that is going on behind the scenes.

It's easy to sit back and feel like others had opportunities that maybe you didn't, but instead I encourage you to be prolific and proactive. First, decide what you want. Yes, it sounds so simple, but it's undeniable that you will get to where you want to go faster if you have a more accurate map. Let this become your blueprint for life. I will tell you that in order to get to your final destination, you will need to learn how to *Stand Alone*.

BREAKING OUT OF THE CAGE

Sometimes in life, you don't know exactly what you're doing or the next right choice to make. But when you look back later on, everything was always connected and pushed you to the next step along your journey. To Stand Alone, you must first decide that you're going to be amazing at whatever you're doing. Standing Alone is what you get when you mix a monk and a warrior. A monk that loves the silence can reflect and control their emotions so they can respond rather than react. And a warrior that can execute on command has the courage to guard and protect the things that matter the most to them, and the strength to annihilate the enemy. What do you get when you cross a monk and a warrior? *Dangerous.*

This is a manifesto for greatness. Every young girl needs to read this and take it to heart so that they are properly equipped with what it takes to truly succeed in this world. Every young boy needs to read this to grow into a strong man. Every man and woman needs to read this because you are manifesting weakness or strength in your children with your words and actions—and our children are the future.

Most of us today are living in cages. When we are young, we feel like we are in a cage and want to break free from our parents' watch. When they finally release us from this cage, though, have they actually prepared us to deal with the real world? Have they really trained us to survive on our own? Oftentimes, the answer is no. So we end up creating a cage for ourselves and staying in our own comfort zone instead of breaking free and growing into the people we're supposed to be. This happens on a subconscious level, because we do what is familiar to us.

But what if what is familiar is scary? What if familiar is violent and aggressive? What if what is familiar is not safe, but is instead the act of having to find an enormous amount of courage in the midst of great uncertainty? What if what is familiar is not having everything given to us but rather learning how to *hunt* for what we want? What happens to a child that is raised like this versus the child that is raised to be kept safe and secure?

That child is me. What was made familiar to me would destroy most people. My familiar and everyday life was filled with trauma and hardship that I could have let destroy me. However, I decided to overcome it. I decided to push myself to the limit and rise above my circumstances. I know now that without it, I wouldn't be where I am now. Though it was difficult and unpleasant, it helped me to become the person that I am today.

On the other side of everything that makes you feel safe, secure, and familiar is your best life. It's a life that you cannot even imagine having as yours because the cage is capturing your mind and thoughts in order to make you think less and less about what's waiting just outside of it. You become accustomed to a very unnatural way of living: Everything you need is already available to you whenever you need it, and there's often someone telling you what to do all the time. Living this way, you begin to lose the power of your own thoughts, mind, and choices, and you can't think for yourself anymore because you have been told what to do for so long.

How do you know if you are trapped? You feel it in your spirit. God plants a seed inside all of us. When we are not authentic—true to who we really are created to be or put in an environment that doesn't allow us to express fully who we are—we feel it in our spirit. It's why the people around us who really care to support us in finding the greatest version of ourselves are priceless. If not, it feels like we are trapped in a cage. We can anesthetize ourselves by lying to ourselves or settling for less, but all this does is further kill our spirit that want to grow the seed that was planted inside of us from our Creator.

We can only zone into what this unique seed in us is by truly knowing ourselves. When the voice of our spirit inside of us is loud and clear, we start to stop caring about all the voices that make a lot of noise on the outside.

Everyone is different. We all have unique interests and things that we gravitate toward. That's why copying someone is so deadly. It literally kills the seed planted inside of us instead of nurturing who we are called to be. It won't be until this seed is nurtured and fully blossomed that you will feel truly free. That's where all of our freedom lies. When we are able to actualize and express who we were created to be. When we are living in alignment with our design.

Trapped people are easy to identify: They are the teenagers who are engulfed by the noise of social media and the seemingly extravagant lives that everyone posts online, showing everything they have. They are the young adults who have nothing in common with anyone else in their families, who feel so alone with their own thoughts, who wonder what in the world they are doing with their lives. It's the modern woman who is working under the incompetent man she has to report to who continues every day to insult her intelligence. It's the mother who is constantly surrounded by the noise and chatter of her children and begins to feel that she needs to escape or she will go crazy. It's the man who is listening to the noise of the world trying to weaken him and make him more docile until he has no more control over his own life. It could also be the employee who knows he or she is called to be an entrepreneur. Or the entrepreneur who would rather be an employee. We are free when there is no more confusion and we are clear and aligned with who we are called to be. This doesn't come from the outside opinions of others—it's something cultivated from within.

We have all felt this at one time or another. The work begins once we come to the realization that we are trapped and now we must work on breaking free.

What's your cage? That's what Standing Alone is really all about. Leading your life by design, free from the noise of the world telling you want you can and can't do—what you won't or will do. It's you making a decision to accept the responsibility of leading your own life.

It's within the worst things that you will ever go through that you will find the strength and power to create a life filled with the best things that could ever happen to you. Those terrible times really happened *for* you and not to you.

I want to help. I mean *really* help you. Not simply tell you what everyone else is telling you but to actually have the courage to tell you what really needs to be said. What does it take to achieve great levels of success? Being a nice person isn't enough. Do you have the stomach juices to quietly sit there in the middle of a storm and execute violently in order to create the life you want to live? Everyone is selling you something, but a seller needs a buyer. What are you buying? Are you buying into this story that you already have everything you need to succeed? Or do you feel like something just isn't right…like something is missing?

Why do they tell you to stay where you are and be patient, while they manipulate their way to the top? Trusting the process only works when you're being led by the right people, not cowards who are looking to keep their title and position and really only care about buying more time so they can beef up their pension.

I am not playing a small game, so I don't expect to win the small prizes. I want it all.

But I know what it will take in order to make that happen. I have been trained to go to war since I was a little child, and I still train. Every. Single. Day. When you get to where I am, you will be able to see where I was and where you once were. I know that I haven't scratched the surface of what I am capable of doing, so every day I wake up and the claws come out. I know what it feels like to be at the bottom in the dark, looking up, wanting to get out. I know what it feels like to not have any money to eat. I know what it feels like to sleep on the floor because a mattress is a luxury. It's not about someone throwing you a rope. It's not about someone coming to rescue you. It's about you learning how to claw yourself out, one millimeter at a time. It's about looking at any daunting task and growing the balls that you don't have to overcome the fear that rises up inside all of us. To kill the voice that says, "Just stay put, be safe, and don't take risks, because it's too dangerous!" Do you know what's dangerous? *You are.* Are you training like no one else? Are you willing to do what no one else is willing to do? Are you willing to claw your way out millimeter by millimeter? You would if you knew that you would make it to the other side. You would if you knew what was waiting for you. It's time for you to start clawing and finally arrive, because your best life is waiting on the other side.

God is perfect; God doesn't make mistakes.

Everything in your life is in perfect working order to get you to Stand Alone and carve out the best version of yourself. Whatever pain and suffering you are enduring—be thankful for it. It's been placed in your life on purpose. Like the seed that is sitting under the pounds of dirt that has to find the strength to push against the downward pull of life, to fight and come up to find the light and air to breathe—all those pounds of dirt is the pressure that's on you. The only way to get to the light is to push against the downward pull of life and in doing so you find more energy, more creativity, more of everything good. You have developed the muscle, the courage, to fight the good fight.

That's what this book is all about. Making you know without a shadow of a doubt that you will make it out. You will make it out of that dark hole and find yourself in the light one day. You will see that no one and nothing will ever scare you again. You will start to gain control over the voices that speak to you to keep you safe. It's not about being safe. It never has been. Movement is life. There is no great victory that you will ever experience without the pain of discipline. The discipline to keep moving and keep clawing. Never give in. Never give up. Victory is yours.

And every millimeter that you claw through will be a deposit that you make into yourself. It will give you the confidence to deal with much greater things in the future. We are all training for that next level. Even in our death, we will come to terms with what we are and what we could have been. My question to you is: What will your next level be? We are all working towards gaining this. Victory is calling. Will you answer?

Live your life like you would rather die a hero than live like a coward. The world has enough cowards. This is your calling—to be a hero. And the first person you have to save is yourself. Every single thing that has ever happened to you or that is happening to you now is designed to make you stronger so that you can outplay and outlast everyone around you. Let every experience teach you. Strong is having the courage to connect and disconnect from the right people and choose your environment. Strong is being intelligent and reading data and recognizing what is happening in the right way to serve you, not destroy you.

> *"Never give in. Never give in. Never, never, never, never—in nothing, great or small, large or petty—never give in, except to convictions of honour and good sense. Never yield to force. Never yield to the apparently overwhelming might of the enemy."*
>
> *—Winston Churchill*

CALM LIKE A MONK; ALERT LIKE A WARRIOR

Do you really think you were brought into this world to be defeated? Do you not see the miracle that you are? The weakest version of you already died. For you to exist, there was the greatest race that was ever won. It was an obstacle course that was all upstream and no easy feat. One sperm had to fight off between 40 to 150 million other versions of you. It was under a tremendous amount of pressure to do this. There was a time limit to get to the end—the egg—or the sperm would have died off. Barriers to entry make us stronger. After that major victory, you still had to be nurtured. Think of all the chemical processes that had to take place just before you arrived.

As infants pass through the birth canal, they undergo an enormous amount of stress. Imagine being in this high-pressure and stressful environment and growing into it. It's normal for you. You probably heard the saying that "Warriors are made." When we hear this, we think we are all weak and fragile and strength has to be created. I disagree. You came out of the womb a warrior. You have to remember who you are. You have to work every day to reinforce the warrior that's lying dormant underneath the surface. When they say a warrior is made, remember who made you. Do you think God can even create someone weak and broken? Life hits some of us really hard sometimes, and in those moments, you need to pull out the warrior that's already inside of you. Remember how you entered this world. The sound of water. The darkness. The sound of her heartbeat put us in and out of sleep. All of a sudden, the water broke. Hormones changed, and it was like we instinctively knew that we needed to move. We needed to get out. The baby knows to push his head through the canal. The baby is squashed as the contractions force the baby to move down further. The baby is receiving less oxygen from the mother's constricting blood vessels, less oxygen being given to the umbilical cord. Do you know what most babies do in this high-stress situation? They sleep through it. You came into this world prepared to deal with enormous amounts of stress. In all this stress, what is the best way for the mother to be? The answer is the same when we are in the most stressful situations in our life. Calm, like a monk. The mother's calmness helps the child to be calm and alert. Yes, calm *and* alert. The calmer you are, the more alert you are. You see everything that is happening around you, and you are able to make a better decision at that time. Calm like a monk, alert like a warrior.

As the baby passes through the birth canal, the skull molds itself to its environment to pass through. This is another key to our success. Are you so rigid, fixed, and incapable of change that you can't pass through to the next part of your life? That's why so many people get stuck in their cages. Their inability to change, mold, and reconfigure themselves is the exact thing that keeps them caged and significantly stuck. The first time we experience this liberation from being caged is during the childbirth process. The enormous amount of pressure that the baby feels actually helps it to breathe as it forces the lungs to expel fluid and mucus and prevents the ingestion of any other substances as the baby passes through the canal. Maybe that's why we feel like we can't breathe when we are under enormous amounts of stress. That's why a lot of us have to remind ourselves to calm down and *just breathe* under these circumstances. The greatest challenges that we will face are passing through to the next phase in our life, and it's so symbolic to the ways in which all of our unique lives began.

The same goes for the act of being calm. Being able to maintain a sense of calmness and control—even during highly stressful events—is something that sets us up for success in life and business. Having a temper is just as weak as being soft. It's on the other end of the spectrum. I encourage you to get above the spectrum. Rise above the emotions. Imagine yourself floating above the situation you are in and seeing what really should happen, then choosing what *you* want the outcome to be. I train myself to be calm, and I work at it every day. Being calm doesn't mean you don't care or that you're not using your voice or allowing your opinions to be heard. Being calm means that you see everything clearer and make better decisions. Soft people and hard people are both damaged people. I'm not damaged...I'm healed and stronger than ever before. Every day, I am the best version of myself.

I am not hard. I am not soft. I am what I am. My life will speak for who I am. Let your life speak for who you are. I have learned to detach from my situations in order to see things from a different perspective. As a child, I learned how to do this the first time I made a decision to stand up and physically fight back for my family. I detached from being a little girl, I detached from being a human body so that I could find the superhuman strength to stand up for what was right.

It's only when we detach from ourselves that this power can enter us and rise up within. We tap into something greater than just who we are. That greatness is inside of all of us. Every day, we make a decision to strengthen or weaken its presence by our thoughts, words, and actions. When we fail to feed our stronger self, a weaker version takes over. Humans are emotional beings. The act of detaching from our emotions and rising up takes an ability to step outside yourself that allows you to see more, act better, be more accurate, and be clearer. It's seeing things from another vantage point—really emptying yourself so that you are not weighed down. Weighed down with emotions. Weighed down with fear. Weighed down with the past. Weighed down with overthinking and overanalyzing. That's what paralyzes most people, but not me. My freedom comes from my ability to detach. I detach from my feelings and learned that I can be in control of my emotions instead of my emotions being in control of me. When we learn to control our emotions, we are able to clearly evaluate the whole picture from all perspectives, and then we have the power to choose what our response will be. We stop being reactive and we start to be in control of the situation, and we create the outcome that is beneficial rather than living as a victim of circumstance.

BEING A WOMAN IN BUSINESS

Being a woman in business, you MUST have this skill. You MUST be in control of the switch. The on and off switch of all the people who live within you. The calm monk and the dangerous warrior. Business for women is different. The biggest lie being told is that we are all equal. Women and men are different. We are not equal, nor should you want to be equal to anyone. Want to be better. When you have a child and you are in business as a woman, it will affect you even more differently. I had to learn how to be strong and soft at the same time. Strong as a business warrior operating in a very masculine space but still being the woman who can melt when your son hugs you and says, "I love you, Mom" in the sweetest voice you've ever heard in your life. That's why women don't understand just how powerful they are or can become. They often see softness as weakness, and it's not. It's your innate strength. Let your softness make you more hard.

I force myself to use those female strengths to pave a path that allows me to achieve more. We need more female leaders, but to have that, females need to see more women in leadership positions so that it becomes believable. We need to understand that it's possible to use our womanly characteristics and traits in order to strengthen us as leaders in the business world.

It's essential to learn to detach and not be afraid to control your emotions and personalities. The goal is to make our emotions become fluid and move seamlessly with us in total control. We appear to be different from other people, but we know we are always the same. We are one with a higher power. It's so important for women to bear down and get through any emotions that can take you out of the game. Learn to see your commitment to your business like a mother commits to her child. I pity the fool who gets in the way of a mother and her children. My business was my first child. I've seen it through a lot of ups and downs. And it's so important to see more women advance so that more women believe that it's possible for them also. You do this by tapping into that innate quality of loving your business like a mother loves a child. You nurture it like no one else. You are deeply connected to it like no one else. Then you will become successful like no one else. Use all these emotions inside of you to make you stronger.

That's how successful teams work, with many individuals melting into one. Moving and working as one unit but with each individual having their own unique role and responsibility for the team. You can trust that everyone will do their part, that no one wants to do someone else's part. But we all know that we can if we are called to. True strength comes from the bonds, like atoms. That's where all the power and strength lie. That's why when you want to break or conquer someone, you first have to break them apart or divide them by breaking their bonds. Just like a woman who is a mother, a CEO, a wife, a daughter—we are really only one.

When we are too rigid, we become susceptible to being damaged, like when Bruce Lee said to become the water. Surfers know this. When they are in the ocean, they become one with the waves. They don't see themselves separate—like a surfer on the wave—because that's how the wave can eat them up. Once the surfer sees the wave and separates, he's done. Instead, the wave, which is water, becomes one with the surfer, who becomes water. That's how it becomes a beautiful experience. He is flawless in his movements, acting as one symbiotic being.

When you look at your enemies as separate from you, that's when you allow them to be able to attack you. You can control your enemy when you become them because you know how to control yourself. This is why the first thing you have to learn to control is yourself. Once you become one with yourself, no one else can harm you.

Become ONE with the mind: What you choose to think about, what you choose to enter your mind, and who you allow to enter your mind is what you are becoming.

Become ONE with the body: What you physically do, the sculpting of your outer shell, and the shedding of all the excess, building your body's strength by resistance training helps you to become stronger.

Become ONE with the spirit: Choosing to connect to a spirit that is bigger and stronger than you for unlimited power and extra insight, the gift of discernment, heightened senses and experiences, and better intuition and instincts are key to having sustained success.

In order to step into your full power, you must learn to continuously strengthen and train these three areas in your life. It's not a one-time event. It's a lifetime commitment to becoming extraordinary.

FINDING YOUR POWER

Aristotle said, "Give me a child until he is seven and I will show you the man." There is no doubt that our childhood affects us both positively and negatively. It shapes us and molds our instincts and behaviors. It's possible to override this foundational knowledge, but it's not easy. You must have the ability to see everything you have been through as a child as aiding you to become stronger, rather than making you become weak and a victim of circumstance. The choice is yours. And that is where all your power lies. Choose to see everything that happened to you as things that are now helping you. And continue to do so as you grow through life instead of just going through life.

If I had the parents I wanted, I would never be who I am today. There are so many things that I did deep work on to bring you this information. I understand that my parents did everything they could do for me—and it was perfect. They did their best. They were perfect for me, and I'm very grateful for everything and every opportunity that they gave to me. Looking back, I see how it was perfect for me because I am able to Stand Alone and stand apart in my life right now.

My childhood was anything but perfect. I felt at times that I was living in a small hell. I love it today because it made me who I am. I was able to navigate my way out, and instead of being a victim of my upbringing and surroundings, I became a person who is equipped to conquer. I was raised by toughness, and we play as we practice.

> *"If the world hates you, keep in mind that it hated me first. If you belonged to the world, it would love you as its own. As it is, you do not belong to the world, but I have chosen you out of the world. That is why the world hates you." (John 15:18–19)*

It's OK if everyone doesn't understand you. Not everyone has seen what you have seen and been through what you have been through. Not everyone has what you have inside of you. Work on your internal being and foundation of who you are, and remember that the outside world won't always agree with you. It will require that you Stand Alone in order to get to where you want to go.

When I was younger, I cared so much about fitting in. I wanted to dress like my friends, and I wanted to shop where they shopped. Blending in was always my goal. I didn't want to be different. Every kid is like this at some point, but when I look back at my adolescent and childhood years, I was always making the choice to separate myself from the pack. While it's normal to want to fit in, I also think that a lot of people are dying inside because we are feeling more and more forced to comply rather than taking a stand or going against what everyone else is doing. Some of us have this innate feeling of who we are and what we stand for, even at a very young age. It's difficult then to go along with what everyone else wants us to do, or say, or wear. When you are different, it's challenging to try to fit the mold of what everyone else wants you to be. But if you choose not to Stand Alone, parts of yourself start to diminish and die over time. This feeling can be felt even when we're young children just trying not to stand out to our peers, classmates, and even families.

When I was in high school, I felt this a lot. I was friends with everyone (that's the Canadian in me), but I was also able to differentiate what was right from what was wrong. My exposure to different groups made me realize where I wanted to end up. There was a group of girls that would dress a certain way with baggy pants sagging down and big T-shirts. I remember I would always do my shopping in the States when we lived in Canada. We would get clothes that no one could get in Canada, and I loved this. I remember the girls and guys calling me Flamingo because I have a high waist and I actually wore my pants where they were supposed to be. I could have easily decided to dress like they were dressing to fit in, but that actually would have made me even more uncomfortable. (I probably wouldn't have even been allowed to dress how they dressed, to be perfectly honest.) But I loved dressing up. I always loved makeup and fashion. I remember one day waiting for the bus and the "ringleader" of that crowd came up to me and asked me where I got all my clothes. I told her in the States when we go visit family, and she said she really liked my shoes.

Here's the point: while you are busy trying to blend in, to wear what everyone else is wearing, there is a leader who thinks about being different. They aren't thinking about fitting in. Instead, they actually admire people who do the opposite and have their own style. When you have this feeling that you are doing something just because everyone else is, you actually feel like you are dying inside when you are a leader—because you are. Leaders have something inside that tugs at them. They want to win. They want to be in the front. They want to dominate. WE WANT TO LEAD AND MAKE AN IMPACT!

When you don't feed this and you are blending in instead of standing out, it feels like we are dying inside. It's not a sudden death, but slowly and surely, you are suffocating who you really are in service to being a second-rate someone else. This is why leaders despise copying. The greatest leaders are innovators. We know that we can model success to a point and then we have to start creating. We start to stand out instead of blending in and being average.

That doesn't mean that leaders are the most loud or the most visually dominant. You don't have to be the biggest or the loudest in the room to be the best leader. Great leaders understand that we influence with our confidence. Our confidence comes from doing great work. We can be quietly out-working everyone else and not care that no one notices because we know that we are building skill and in a process to create greatness. Leaders understand that the deepest work isn't always seen—it's what we do in the dark when no one else is watching that separates us from the pack. Leaders are in tune to the voices within themselves. That's why you must learn that the most important person who you must learn to lead is yourself before you attempt to lead others. The best leaders lead themselves constantly. The worst leaders don't lead themselves and bark orders and demands at everyone else.

STANDING OUT

I never really fit in anywhere. I was and still am the black sheep in my family. Growing up, I was friends with some people who did some not-so-great things like stealing, doing drugs, and acting sexually promiscuous. At the same time, I had friends who were gifted. I had taken many tests to see if I was gifted. According to those tests, I wasn't gifted scholarly, but I was above average. As it turns out, I was gifted in many other things, like decision making. Another gift was my ability to watch what other people were doing and being able to walk away from crowds that I knew wouldn't serve me.

> *"You must be confronted with an ethical dilemma—a choice between one road that is rocky, steep, and treacherous and the other that is smooth, flat, and comfortable. One road tests your fortitude, the other provides an easy path. One is filled with temporary hardships and pain, the other is quick and easy. But in the end, if you choose the harder path less traveled, the path where the virtuous have walked, the journey will make you stronger, more resilient, and more capable of conquering the other steep climbs on your way to the top. While the second path, the easy way, will leave you unprepared for the future challenges of life."*
>
> *—Admiral William H. McRaven*

Growing up, I never sought advice from anyone. I wouldn't read this quote until much later in my life when I started to dive into self-development and high performance. What I can tell you is that high performers are not interested in fitting in. They are most interested in forging the greatest version of themselves. Every time I made a decision, a hard decision, to walk away and choose the more difficult path, what I didn't know was that I was developing the leader in business that I would one day be. I was building the muscles to make the hard work easier in the future.

Every time we choose the smoother and more comfortable pathway, we weaken ourselves. This doesn't change as you get older—it just becomes more obvious. It's the person who eats whatever tastes good rather than eating what is necessary for the body to function at optimal levels. It's the person who wakes up in the morning with no time to plan and prepare or put anything good inside of them rather than train their physical body, put the stress on the muscles so that they grow and support a strong body, so they become soft by default.

This rings true in life and in our careers. In business, I wanted to be the best more than I wanted to fit in. Sure, it would've been nice if everyone liked me, but I quickly realized—just as I did as a kid growing up—that everyone is placed in my life to provide me with alternative paths to choose. Not everyone is an example. Some people are placed in our lives as a warning. Remember that.

I'm glad when I was growing up that I never had the pressures of social media or a phone attached to my hand and accessible at all times. Even now, I am very aware of how damaging it is to be a spectator in someone else's life versus being a player in your own life. Being alone without the constant bombardment of constant communication through the cell phone, social media, and news helps to me to think. All these mediums in our lives are noise that distracts us. We have to be able to unplug and focus. It doesn't mean you need a vacation—you can do this at work. Whatever you are doing, do it without distraction. These times of total focus sharpen our skills. I call this deep work. This allows me to get away in my mind and actually listen to what feels right and wrong inside of me, rather than the constant bombardment of images and soundbites and quotes by which most people have been overwhelmingly influenced. It allows me to go deeper. It allows me to enjoy being alone. Spending time alone may be one of the hardest things to do in today's world, but I can't recommend anything more. Get comfortable being alone. Listen to the voice that is deep within you. Quiet all the noise of the world and learn to channel who you really are and what you are destined to become. When you practice this daily, it becomes easier. You start to realize what a powerful tool you already possess: the ability to *think*. This is how you start to influence rather than be influenced all the time.

For so long, I wanted people to like me until I realized this really makes no difference in my life. I need to have the *right* people appreciating and respecting me. In business, there were no women who were where I wanted to be. I had to learn from men. I looked to these men for guidance until I realized that they are broken also. The truth is, we are all imperfect, insecure, and afraid. I came to understand that no one knows exactly what they are doing. Everyone is figuring it out along the way. Even the best leaders are still testing and trying to see what works and what doesn't. No one has all the answers. In fact, the moment when you feel like you have all the answers is when you become a liability.

Instead of idolizing these men and trying to be like them, I listened to their experiences and appreciated the wisdom that they had learned through the years of being in business. I am grateful to every single one of them who spent time with me to nurture me through the years and the many hardships that I have endured.

People always ask me who my hero is. No human is my hero. I don't idolize anyone. I've met some really amazing people in my lifetime. I've spoken to some of the strongest people on planet earth, though I'm not mesmerized by people. At one point in my life, I looked up who the hardest man on the planet was, and I had him coach me for a year and a half. It was one of the greatest experiences I had because he made me realize what I already knew. He reminded me who I was because of what I have been through and overcome. It was a confirmation process for me. I know that everyone is human. What impresses me is the power of the human spirit and the ability to overcome. Too many people are admiring others instead of working on themselves. It's so easy to do that today. You go on social media, and everyone looks perfect and seems like their lives are flawless, though absolutely no one has a perfect life. All that you have the power to do is simply work on yours. All the attention that you give to other people by admiring them...instead, choose to put that attention into your own life. Start harnessing that attention for building your faith. My faith comes from my belief in a higher power, and I deeply trust that my life is guided. Everyone that comes into my life, good or bad, is there to teach me something new about myself that I've yet to learn—or sometimes remind me who I am.

STARTING OUT (THE NEW GIRL)

When you get into business and you are new, it's really easy to get mesmerized by people and think they are so amazing. I see a lot of females do this with males, and it leads to very unhealthy scenarios. Know that they only look amazing now because of all those years of hard work and training. Ladies, save the batting of the eyelashes and get ahead by putting in the work and developing your skills. That's how you will become respected. The truth is that there are a lot of people in higher positions who are not really good at what they do. If you work on your skills and never lose yourself in the process, you can become the person who many people respect and want to listen to as well.

You would be amazed at how many people who are in senior positions in companies really have no clue what they are doing. I don't say this to be disrespectful—I say this to be inspiring. In fact, the greatest people can admit the fact that they are still figuring it out. The more you are trying to achieve, the more uncertain you will be because you are always doing something new. Innovators are quite comfortable living in this state of uncertainty.

When I started in insurance, I was still the kind of person who was concerned about what other people thought. The greatest gift was that God took all my family and friends away from me. I never knew why I was cast out from my family. Though I know now that if I was speaking to my family at that time, I would never have made it. I would have cared too much about what they thought. Their opinions don't pay my bills. The truth is, no one's opinions pay your bills, but we give so much unnecessary weight to what other people think. You become truly free when you are able to quiet the noise of other people's opinions and learn to seek wise council instead of someone to console you and your problems. There is a very big difference between surrounding yourself with people who can help to guide you with better quality information versus just talking to someone to gain comfort and agreement. I caution you with this because until you become very certain about who you are and what you are looking to achieve, with absolute certainty, you will have a tendency to get off track and distracted by the noise of someone else's opinion. Some people can even come from a place of loving you and still end up hurting you. You have to learn to have the gift of discernment. Assess who is speaking to you and what it is that they stand to gain or lose in helping you. Are you both aligned with the same goals and mission? I believe in total alignment. When a family, a team, a couple, are totally aligned and want the best outcome together and there are no hidden agendas, you can create an atmosphere of trust. This is why faith is so important also—faith in leadership, faith in your team, faith in systems. Faith in a higher power beyond myself has been the guiding light through all my difficulties. Living a life based on principles and values rather than convenience is what will help to propel you to the top. And life will present moments where you get to practice choosing your principles and values over what is just easier to do. And every time you do this, you will start to notice that you feel better about yourself. It will get easier and easier. We live in a world where everybody wants everything faster and faster. Remember this:

your life is not an Amazon delivery. Doing the right thing will always serve you better than doing what is convenient. I've never met anyone who took a shortcut and was happy about it in the end. Learning to think for yourself and running what people present to you against your own principles and values is always better. This is what character is: our ability to do the right thing when we think no one is watching. The truth is you are always watching you, and I believe my Creator is watching me. Learn to quiet the noise of the outside world and get properly aligned with environments and people that are in support of your principles and values.

How do you know if your principle and values are correct? It will show up in your results eventually, and they will align with people who have accomplished more. Success leaves clues. People who are very successful from all types of industries hold similar values and principles. For example, I don't know a single successful person in business who doesn't highly value work ethic—your ability to work hard. There might be some cool Instagram post that you read from some unemployed guy living in his mom's basement that said, "Work smart—not hard." But all really successful people know that's not true. You have to put in the work. There is no getting out of it. There are no shortcuts to winning in the long run. Skills are accumulated through repetition, and that takes time. If you don't value working hard, it will be very hard for you to give your absolute all to what it is that you are doing.

CHAPTER 1

Why You MUST Stand Alone to Become Who You Were Destined to Be

S TANDING ALONE IS about being able to withstand the pressures that all of us face in pursuit of the greatest version of ourselves.

Where does the confidence come from in someone who can find courage in the face of their enemy? The confidence to say or do something they really don't want to do, but they know that they must do it? The confidence to withstand the enormous amount of peer pressure that every child will face growing up? The confidence to go through enormous amounts of rejection and still find the courage to keep on going? To take the harder path, to do the task that is more challenging rather than choose the path of least resistance? Where does someone find the discipline to choose the harder path that will give them a long-term gain rather than the person who chooses the quick fix, which will ultimately lead them to a worse-off position?

Standing Alone is about building the endurance and the grit that it takes to forge a better version of yourself. It's the version that's taken hold of your own power, the version that would forever remain hidden under the surface, the version that wants to come out and drive you to level up your entire life. So many people die with a multitude of regrets because they fuel their fears instead of feeding their courage. This book is about something every human being has to face at one point or another in our lives: Will we remain the same, by settling, or can we drive ourselves to become the greater version of who we are meant to be, the version that is dying to break through into the light?

These aren't scenarios that I have made up. They are happening all the time to all of us. You aren't alone…and I'm not alone, either. The act of Standing Alone has nothing to do with actually being by yourself. When I look back at my own foundations, I always turn to my faith. With this, I have never felt completely alone. Even in times of difficulty, I've always known that there is a guiding light over me that allows me to hold onto great faith and trust. This pushes me to do my best, and having it gives me the strength to Stand Alone without feeling like I'm out by myself doing something scary. But you must learn how to Stand Alone in the way that I do in order to get the right outcome. There are certain laws that govern our universe, and there is an order to everything. Understand that for every decision you make, you are generating the response by the choice and path you choose to take. How do we come to know these things? How does someone gain this wisdom and insight? It's always through the act of Standing Alone. The hardest answers you will find in your life will come from you, when you do the ultimate face-off of your current self versus the person you know deep down inside you are destined to become.

Standing Alone happens in the dark, when you are by yourself. It could be that you are surrounded by so many other people, but maybe you don't fit in. Standing Alone is about not fitting in but separating ourselves. When you feel like you are the lone wolf, the maverick, the black sheep in the family, you are done with attempting to fit in and please other people. Know you are on the journey to become who you were really meant to be. This is one of the hardest decisions that you will ever confront. No one will understand why you are doing what you are doing, but you do it anyway because you know it's right for you. They don't have to understand it. You stop caring about the opinions of others, and you visit the darkest places within yourself to discover why you have gone through everything you have been through and reveal the person it has been preparing for you to become. Even if you are surrounded by a lot of noise, you know how to separate yourself from that noise and not let it distract you from your higher goal and purpose.

In the beginning, there was darkness. Everything that came after the darkness was created. In the darkness, this is where we find ourselves. This is where creation occurs. This is where creativity lies. This is where you start to lead your life rather than let life just happen to you. Most people today aren't really living. They are barely existing because they lost hold of who they really are, and they are so busy observing others and becoming a spectator to someone else's life rather than the player in their own. When you are authentically you—the best version of yourself—you will feel a deep sense of freedom. A freedom that has nothing to do with title, position, how much money you possess, or how anyone else sees you. It's a freedom like no other. Before we will ever experience this freedom, there is a stage of suffering that we will have to endure.

Have you ever been in a room so dark you couldn't see your hands right in front of your own face? With time, your senses will change and adjust to the darkness. Your senses will deepen and heighten at the same time. You hear things that you once couldn't hear. The sound of the wind is created by the slightest movement of your body. You feel things that you once couldn't feel. The tiny hairs on your body begin to raise, which gives you increased sensations. Your focus is incredible. Your situational awareness is like that of an animal in the wild hunting for its prey. When you are dark and empty, you are more in tune. In tune to what? To who you are. To what really matters to you. In the dark is where you find the person that you are supposed to be, the person that God intended you to be to begin your fullest form. Then when you get around other people, all the noise—traffic, music, voices, opinions, people's agendas—you start to tune this out because you know how to go to this place because you aren't afraid of the dark. In the dark is deep silence. There isn't the noise of the opinions of others—there are only the voices of those who truly matter to you.

Where is the dark? All of us experience the dark in different ways. It may creep up on us in a certain season in our life where nothing seems to be going our way. It may come unexpectedly. The death of a loved one, an accident that changes everything, a relationship that is broken, a feeling of depression or anxiety that can overtake you. This season is the winter of our lives. We can choose to wallow, or we can choose to make a comeback. It is not easy. It requires spending time with yourself and reexamining what is important to you. What matters to you? What do you want? What price are you willing to pay for what you want? And most importantly, are you willing to commit to achieving this?

Every day is an opportunity to massively change the direction of your life. You must do this on purpose. Never lose hope. Change isn't easy, but it's happening around us and to us all the time. In the outside world, change happens gradually and slowly, so we don't really feel it. When we grow through these periods of darkness, it will take us putting ourselves through a more dramatic shift. A shift in the way we think, the way we see ourselves and the outside world. We must learn to reframe everything, and our understanding must become deeper than what we are currently going through at the time. As we walk through the dark, we understand that we are being guided and we will come out stronger and better than before.

> *Psalms 23:4–5*
> *Even though I walk*
> *through the darkest valley,*
> *I will fear no evil,*
> *for you are with me;*
> *your rod and your staff,*
> *they comfort me.*
> *You prepare a table before me*
> *in the presence of my enemies.*
> *You anoint my head with oil;*
> *my cup overflows.*

Sometimes the circumstances of life thrust us into the dark, and then we have times where we place ourselves in it to constantly improve ourselves. When you are seeking to perform at the highest levels, you will need to be able to place yourself in situations where you can isolate yourself to constantly remind yourself of what is important and to keep yourself on your path to becoming the greatest version of yourself. Some people fast, some people go on retreats to get away and clear their mind, some people meditate; professional athletes train by themselves religiously in their gym before they train with their teammates to give themselves an edge. For me, as a mother of three, it's really hard to find this time for myself, so I wake up very early to invest the time into creating my life instead of letting life happen to me. When you wake up in the morning, do you wake up with just enough time to barely make it to work, or do you carve out space in your day to direct your day, which will help you to direct your life?

For me it's 4:00 a.m., before the sun. Every day. No phone, no social media. I read things that increase my faith and help me to find the answers that are lurking in my mind. I fill up with enough good so that what I encounter in the day through work or my family life cannot deplete me. I see this happen a lot. People give so much of themselves to their work, or to other people, and they don't have a system to recharge themselves. They end up resenting their work, or other people, because they feel so empty. It's not the work or other people that's draining you completely—it's you failing to refuel yourself.

Work has been a savior to me, and I strongly believe that work can be a blessing to us all. When we can dedicate ourselves to a worthy cause and build something that can outlast us, it gives us energy, and it can be a great source of meaning and purpose in our lives when our work feeds our calling. We forget about the time that we are putting in because we are more focused on the goal and vision that we are looking to achieve. We find ourselves in a state of flow where work often doesn't feel like work. It's who we are. That doesn't mean that you won't have bad moments, days, or seasons, but you get through them and you come out stronger. When I was going through a period of great uncertainty in my life and had just moved to a new country and started a new career, I totally immersed myself into my work so that I could remain as productive as possible. It kept my mind off of my current situation, which was really scary at the time and placed a lot of pressure on me. Pressure doesn't break us. Pressure reveals what's really inside of us, and in that moment of pressure, we allow for what is normally suppressed to come out for others to see. Life will squeeze all of us. When we get squeezed through pressure, what's inside of it comes out. A person who isn't religiously putting good inside of themselves will be revealed with life squeezes them, and they will not like what they see. This is why people quit. This is why people run away instead of confronting the issue at hand. They are running away from facing what is being revealed. They blame other people, outside circumstances, but it's them.

For many people, we end up creating a lot of unnecessary dark moments in our lives when we don't apply ourselves or move towards something more positive in the future. Like a goal, or a vision. These things help us keep moving forward instead of living in the past. We must visit the past of our lives and learn from it, but we don't need to live there. Leave the past in the past, once you have done the hard work of examining it and how it was designed to serve you, not to destroy you. People who live in the past end up missing out on what is happening now. They are also very unhappy. The present is about being grateful for the past and gaining the forward movement into the future; our happiness lies in the present, and it's a choice that we have to make. Happiness is not something anyone or anything else can give to us. The nice things in life can surely bring us temporary happiness, but eventually, this wears off. Just like the newness of a new love—if we don't commit to making a decision to be happy, it's only natural that we focus on what is negative and wrong. All of the great injustices are in the past. The more you dwell on this, the more it grows. We have not inserted the past into the present, and it will affect our future. It can become debilitating. Learn to let the past go and create a new outcome. Be self-aware that negative is natural and positive takes effort. Our brain is literally wired as a survival mechanism to point out what is wrong and what is negative in our world. A lazy mind is a negative mind. It takes discipline and constant effort to see the good and constantly make a decision to override what is normal and ordinary in the pursuit of the extraordinary.

Once you have learned to live in the dark, once you have learned to conquer the dark, the dark doesn't own you—you own it and everything else in your world. You can generate control of your response to life on command. There is great peace here. You are familiar with this place, where most people get scared and run away. In the stillness, you know who you are. In the stillness, you know what you believe. This is where your conviction lies. This is where your conviction grows and gets stronger. Not stubbornness—conviction. This is where the truth lives. It's the truth about you and all your weaknesses. This is where the real you lies. Not the person who you portray or pretend to be with to everyone else—the *real* you. And until you start working on *this* person, you can't be living at your highest potential.

Your convictions are discovered and given life in the dark, just like an embryo that rests in the womb. It's where the most chaos exists. It's where resistance lives. Standing Alone is about leading your life and taking it a step beyond just living your life in a daily routine. Most people are simply living and letting life happen to them instead of taking control. Often, they tend to live on the surface of what they are actually capable of doing and becoming. They focus on what other people see rather than working on what they see about themselves. I have learned with time that life doesn't just happen... life happens just. My mother always used to say to me, "Nothing happens overnight." There is real genius in this statement. We think when something happens it's about that moment. If it's good, we tell that person they are lucky. If it's bad, we call them unfortunate. No, it's been building up. There is great wisdom to be understood in the laws of sowing and reaping. This is also the law of cause and effect. Life isn't just happening—it's being created by what we tolerate and permit in our lives. Who and what we tolerate becomes our environment, and our environment shapes us. When you Stand Alone, you examine all of this. When you understand nothing just happens, you look at things differently. You understand the control is in the present and it's all in our response. How will we respond to what is happening? This is our responsibility. The ability to respond instead of reacting. We can respond with faith instead of reacting out of fear. When we find the certainty that everything is working for us, we choose to do what is right rather than play the games that everyone else is playing. Your life isn't a game; It was designed, and it's up to us to fulfill what we were created to be.

What doesn't make sense at the time will make complete sense one day. You will see all of the things that once had you very puzzled turn into puzzle pieces, and you will start to see those pieces come together to create the picture of your life. Everything will start to connect like tiny dots, aligning to create the great masterpiece of your life. When I look back on my own life, I can see now see how all of the experiences led me to exactly where I am today. Maybe I didn't understand or enjoy everything as it was happening, but I am now grateful for everything—the good and the bad—because it pushed me to find where I am today. Instead of manipulating pieces to fit in where you want to fit, your life starts to beautifully and masterfully fall into place. When you see it come together, it will give you a great sense of joy and satisfaction. This happens only when you choose to Stand Alone.

But until then, it will feel like you are walking through hell.

You will feel like you have been forgotten, neglected, abandoned. Standing Alone is a very lonely place to be when you first do it. But as you continue to walk through this hell, you will find yourself walking towards heaven. Heaven—the freest place to be. Life exists in opposites. For every action, we know there is an equal and opposite reaction. That means the intensity of the pain that we feel guarantees that same level of intensity of joy and satisfaction in a distant time that is not of our knowing. Maybe that's the test. The test of who can endure until our time comes for the opposite of what we have endured. What is absolute is that if we pay the price, we will get the promise. When the price we pay is so great we cannot bear the pain and anguish, we must Stand Alone. Everyone else would quit; everyone else would give up. Not you, not me. We continue to advance, no matter how painful it is, and then we collect our prize.

Standing Alone is about not reacting to our emotions and feelings—it's about rising above them. We don't have to be our feelings. We can learn to lead our feelings instead of allowing our feelings to lead us. You must learn how to feel your feelings and not bottle them up or suppress them. Whatever we suppress will appear in another form somewhere else in our lives. Energy cannot be created or destroyed—it is transferred from one form to another. So we must learn to transform our feelings of pain into fuel. Learn to control your feelings and transform them instead of them controlling you and making you be somewhere you are not supposed to be. Remember the darkroom where you can't see anything. Fear is the normal first response, but when you are able to Stand Alone, you rise above what is currently happening. You embrace your fear, confront it head-on. Then you can start to choose your response. You manipulate fear into fuel instead of having fear manipulate you. When fear manipulates you, you start to compromise. You negotiate with the lesser version of yourself. You give up on what you are called to be. You start giving yourself reasons why it's OK to quit. You see yourself as a victim, and you use the excuse of survival for your poor decision making. You react and lose control. How do I know about this? My life has put me in some pretty interesting situations where I have developed a greater insight because I choose to do the deeper work. I have watched others that spin out of control because of their inability to gain control of their emotions. We must chose to do the work that most won't do so we can get to a place where most can't.

I was forced into dark places, and I'm very grateful for it. What I know is that until you go to this place, you are not living at your fullest potential. You are only scratching the surface of what you are capable of achieving.

These times of great hardship and suffering come into our lives to serve us. The level of pain and suffering will differ from person to person, but it exists for all of us. Embrace it. When you embrace it, you go through a metamorphosis. This deep and profound change that you will endure will transform you. You can't change following the masses and listening to everyone's opinions about you. You can't do it because someone told you to do it. You must learn to quiet the noise. Stand Alone so you can stand apart and go where very few have gone. Success is rare. That's why you have to be rare to achieve it. For you to get to where you want to go, you will need to be able to Stand Alone. You have to do the work. No one can do it for you. Are you willing to go through hell to get to heaven? This is what it really takes. No one will tell you this because they want to sell you the dream. They want you to be motivated to buy what they're selling. They want to sell you the easiest path with the least amount of work. They want to sell you the "one thing" or the "five steps." There is no one thing and there are no five steps. It's all you. You have to submit your whole self to the grueling and painful journey of tapping into what's really inside of you. When you are in the pursuit of transforming your life from ordinary to extraordinary, there is no dabbling. It will take you being totally immersed in what you are doing. Most people don't get this, and most people won't understand when you are going through this. They will say things to you like, "Don't you have enough?" or "You work too much." They don't understand it isn't about the stuff, it isn't about the money—it's about your pursuit for the greatest version of yourself.

The best thing you can do is truly know who you are. There isn't anything on the outside that can motivate you to become this specific version of yourself. This deeper desire comes from somewhere within.

Motivation is the lie that makes you quit at the first obstacle that you encounter, but motivation is all about your feelings. All motivation can do is get you started. It's like a jump start that we all need. But motivation will not keep you going. You have to be willing to learn, to put in the time to develop skill, to be open to feedback that maybe you are not that good and you need to get better. That's why so many people are so lost today because they are constantly seeking motivation—so they can start, but they can't finish. When the motivation runs out, mastery has to take its place. Mastery is what lasts. Mastery doesn't happen from watching a video—it's created by working consistently day and night on your craft. Being great is about you rising above your feelings and doing what no one else is willing to do, no matter how you feel.

Very few are willing to Stand Alone because of what it will demand of you. Are you?

CHAPTER 2

Why Women Have a Hard Time Being Violent in Their Execution in Business

U NTIL MY EARLY twenties, I was studying to be a doctor. At the age of nineteen I had a falling out with my parents. I was forced to navigate through life on my own. I had to pay my way through school and work full time with zero financial aid or assistance. After graduating from university, I was forced to take a different career path. If you have immigrant parents like me, you can relate to what that meant: I decided not to listen to them, to leave an agreed-upon medical career, and to go into sales. When my parents turned their backs on me, I was on my own. That was the first time in my life that I wasn't concerned about what anyone in my family thought of me. They disowned me, but it didn't affect me. I say this to you not for your pity but because ultimately this part of my life was a blessing in disguise. My family disowning me forced me to face myself and my own life by myself for the first time. There was no one to fall back on and no one to rely on. For the first time in my life, I had to learn how to survive on my own. It was the scariest and greatest thing that could have ever happened to me. I didn't even realize the impact that decision would have on the rest of my life until much later on.

My parents and I are OK now. We have a great relationship now, but when they tell me anything related to my business, I just don't listen to them. They are not equipped to give me advice on that topic, and I have put boundaries there in order for us to have a healthy relationship. When my mom guilt-trips me for working too hard, I am now able to tune her out. If you want to get to the top—I mean the top of the top—this is the attitude that you have to adopt. Stop caring how people feel about you. It is only holding you back. While people in your life may mean well, they will say things that will destroy you. This doesn't mean they are bad people. Some people are bad people who don't want you to succeed, but for the most part, the people who are closest to you want to make sure that you are OK. They are programmed to think of your well-being. Are you safe? Are you secure? Are you taking care of yourself? Are you spending enough time with your family? These are things that ordinary people worry about. Success requires that you step out of this cage of ordinary and walk into the world of driving yourself to the edge of what you really can become. In order to get there, you have to push yourself to the very edge, a place where very few people are willing to go.

This goes for your business life, too. There is bad advice everywhere, and it's even worse when they hide behind a title or a position. Consultants are a perfect example of this. Be very careful who you listen to in business. Everyone's an expert these days. These experts are often full of themselves. They read something out of a book that sounds good and try to get you to execute on it. I've learned that what sounds good in theory doesn't always work in the field. In the military, they have a saying that when the map doesn't match the field, follow the field! YOU are on the field, not them. If someone else is giving you a map to follow, make sure that it aligns with the field that you are actually in. This doesn't mean that you don't ever listen to anyone. Listen to the right people. Sometimes it will take someone to bring to your attention something that you are not seeing. Make sure that someone who is giving you advice is qualified to be giving you that advice.

What have they done? What have they accomplished on their own? Before you listen to someone, make sure that you know who you are listening to. I've seen these "expert" consultants and directors float around from office to office, their noses in the sky, thinking they have all the answers. But take it from me: Never take entrepreneurial advice from someone who has never run a successful business in your same industry. You may think you are being polite. They walk away with a free lunch, and you end up losing thousands—maybe millions—of dollars listening to their bad advice. Their advice might work for someone looking to survive, but it won't help someone looking to do what's never been done. It's important that you have the ability to think for yourself. This is not to get confused with you being coachable and led by people who can actually help you. You have to be able to discern between someone who is just doing their job versus a leader who is actually looking to grow and develop you into a better person. Most people in business who play from a position or title have lost this. The best way to handle these situations is to be upfront and tell them that you appreciate them coming, but you are really busy. They will eventually get the point.

Stop being polite. Business isn't polite—it's ruthless. There's a reason why they say nice guys finish last. In order to get ahead, you have to stop worrying about what others think and say about you behind your back. You need to look out for yourself and not the feelings of everyone around you. Think about it like this. If someone (a family member or businessperson) gives you bad advice and it costs you a ton of money, are they going to cut you a check to make up for your losses? No! So don't listen to bad advice for the sake of being polite. Business simply isn't polite. You need to be able to make your own decisions in order to be direct and confident, and that will only happen once you get into the habit of having the final say in your business. Especially if you are an entrepreneur or leader, the final say is always going to be on you.

This chapter covers why it is so hard for women to adopt this mindset, what has trained us to think about everyone else's needs before our own, and how to break these habits so that you can finally start putting yourself first and not feel guilty about it. This is why very few women rise to the highest ranks of leadership because if you're not prepared for this life, then you'll have feelings that it isn't right. You're walking into a man's world, but you don't have to lose who you are as a woman.

When the little boy was playing football and learning about offense and defense, being physically tackled to the ground, and the parents were screaming at him to GET UP—training him to take the hits and keep on going, what was the little girl doing? Was she sheltered? Was she spoken to like a little princess who could do no wrong? If the little girl wasn't competing in something and being molded to win by her parents, when these two meet up years later in the boardroom, who do you think is going to win? The answer is simple: the one who is better prepared.

How many of us have heard that women are too emotional? Well, did anyone ever wonder why that is? Women have developed this evolutionary mechanism to be hyperaware of danger when the man was away and the woman had to guard her family. How many of us have heard to never mess with a woman's intuition? Why is that? Because when we were picking berries, we had to discern what was okay to eat, and we had to speak to people in the communities and find out more information to give our family an advantage. We can hear things men can't hear. We can also pick up on things that most men are blind to.

Emotions and intuition. Two of the most powerful drivers of action. If we can learn to harness these qualities instead of allowing them to control our behaviors by making us very reactive, we can learn to dominate. Learn to use them to help you by controlling them instead of them controlling you. Ladies, we must learn to lead our emotions and learn the gift of discernment when it comes to our intuition.

Feelings are nothing more than feelings, and you absolutely have to move past your emotions in business. We are human beings, so of course you will always have feelings. This isn't a bad thing! When you Stand Alone, you start to learn how to control your feelings and have power over your internal emotional state instead of being controlled by it. What is natural isn't always what is right. Disorder and decay are natural, while growth requires work and order. Being in business forced me to tap into a side of myself that I know everyone who is successful in business has to tap into—whether you are a woman or a man, you MUST be able to access this side of yourself that controls the situation instead of being controlled by the situation if you want to experience success and freedom.

I have heard many people say that women are too emotional, and that's why they don't rise up the ranks in business. More and more women are entering the business world, but there is still a major void of women at the highest levels of leadership. These levels have the most say in what is important in business. The highest levels in business are where the people—usually men—set the agenda and the targets and make a predetermination of what the outcome will be. If you want to be respected in the business world, you have to meet people where they are. You don't have to tell them who you are, but show it all through your work. These higher levels of leadership determine the future of the business and where that business will focus and shift its attention to in the future. I think it's very important for women to want to EARN their seats at these tables. I think it's equally important for men to want to have women who EARN their place to be seated at the table with them. I have found that even if a woman earns the right to sit at the table in these high leadership places, if the men are uncomfortable listening to women, it still won't work. It will take men and women learning how to work together to really solve this problem. Women must recognize that no man will respect a woman if she didn't earn the right to be there. And men must recognize that they can stand to learn something from listening to a different point of view instead of just having people around them who always agree with them.

The first mentors I had in business never made me feel like I was a "woman in business." They successfully created an environment where good was good and it didn't have a gender. I was competing with everyone. I have to level up in skill—regardless of gender.

I later found out that I was moved to one team because another manager's viewpoint was "Women don't make it here." Why am I sharing this with you? Because there are "good" men and "bad" men in all businesses. Labelling men doesn't help you get ahead. I was raised by parents who instilled an exceptional work ethic in me. If you are going up against me, you would have to be able to outwork me, which I highly doubt you will be able to do.

And let's be honest—I was never trying to be equal with anyone.

Ladies, are you really equal to them? Not a damn chance. In fact, you need to be ten times better than them before they start to see you as their equal. In terms of emotion, men naturally cope with things differently than females do. I found myself often asking, *What would a man do in this situation? How can I do this differently and compart-mentalize my emotional reactions?* Men don't overthink or overanalyze, and in a business world, you need to possess this quality. Ignorance is not bliss, but if you keep overthinking, someone who just executes more than you will own you. If you make a mistake, you can't over-think it too much. What would a man do? Move on and keep going. They definitely wouldn't be talking to everyone about their mistakes. So ladies, keep going and keep the talking to a minimum. You don't need to publicly discuss your failures with anyone. Good people will accept you no matter what, and your enemies will use them against you. Ladies, while you are thinking about it, simmering in it, delib-erating over it—he's on to the next one. You have to have the ability to keep moving forward and let things go. I personally have learned a lot of these necessary traits from the men around me in work, and this has been so helpful for my own success.

I am not pro-woman and anti-man. I am pro-human. I am for the advancement of all who are good. I believe that everyone should have the equal opportunity to show up and do their best work. However, the only moment that we're very truly equal in opportunity is the moment of creation and then the process of differentiation begins. Men are different from women, and boys are different from girls—that's just a simple fact. What we all do want and deserve is oppor-tunity—giving everyone the chance to earn something. I am who I am within the business world because men (and one woman) molded me...but I do believe that we all have the capacity to learn things of value from one another regardless of gender. I can learn from anyone, even people who I don't always agree with. None of us have all the answers, and it's very limiting to only learn from people who you can relate to or who look like you.

If you're in business and you're a female, learning to navigate through being successful in a man's world is certainly a challenge.

However, you can do it. I did it, and here I am today telling you that it's completely possible for you, as well.

A lot of people don't know how to Stand Alone and lead their own lives. This goes for men just as much as it goes for women. It's a human thing. This isn't about being right. This book is about knowing what it really takes and then going after it. I'm telling you that as a woman in business, you have to be better. You don't play to be anyone's equal. You play to be better. Being a female sets you up to have to show your undeniable greatness. You have to learn to be your very best without apology. Stop acting like a girl if you want to be treated and respected as a woman. That means that you don't have to rant, protest, be unclassy, or hike up your skirt and sell your soul to get where you want to go. There IS another way. I want women to hear the truth. When I hear people talk about business, I often think that's not how it really is. When you see women who rise in the ranks, to these high levels, they have a side to them that says, "Do not cross me." You can smile and look nice but also command full respect. We need more female leaders—we need more women who are undeniably great and more men who are willing to work alongside them.

First, you better make sure that you are damn good at what you do. Your skills need to be on point. If someone is giving you a seat just because you are a female or your skin is a certain color—and not because you bring the goods—that is equally insulting. Success has no gender and no color. Even age is being thrown out of the equation now. Experience and skill are what are real. Second, don't take this personally—but know that it IS personal. What do I mean by this? A lot of people in the positions of leadership in older and more well-established companies can't listen to what you bring to the table. They talk about innovation, but they don't have the means to execute on it. No one will go to bat and fight for your ideas like you. So often, it's easier to just cut you out entirely. Get used to rejection. Don't take it personally, but take it personally so you go back to work and get better. Become undeniably great. If you have a great idea, don't expect everyone to see what you see. Often, people don't have that vision for the future and need proof before they believe. Keep building. Keep moving forward. Never give up on what you see because someone else can't see it.

It's easy for dinosaur companies to keep eating dinosaur food. When presented with new ideas, they aren't going to bite. This is when you have to learn to Stand Alone and DEMONSTRATE through experience. These companies keep working on the same things, same ideas, recycled over and over. They would rather put their time, money, energy, and resources in small, incremental, safe investments than take a chance and listen to someone who can create something bigger and better. Older companies are risk averse. They play for stockholders and not for entrepreneurs. They play for guarantees and not for disruption. They play for security (mainly security of their paycheck, their title, and their chair) and not for freedom. Innovation is not liked.

And that's why they get DISRUPTED.

That's why someone comes along who can Stand Alone and proves them completely wrong. The same idea that they laugh off or scoff at ends up choking them into submission.

Instagram with Kodak.

Netflix with Blockbuster.

Uber with taxis.

Airbnb with hotels.

Crypto with the banking system.

So know this: There has never been a greater time to be in business and to also start thinking like a successful businessPERSON. If you're a woman, why should you learn from men? Simple: because they have been in business longer. Look for examples where men have encountered denial and their ideas have been doubted in their long history of being in the business world. It's a simple fact that men have been in business for longer. Of course, women have also been in business, but in most cases, it's a boys' club that you're walking into as a female leader. Because of this, we sometimes get overlooked; even today, at a conference or a speech, I've had moments when the speaker addresses all the men as a group...they don't even notice you're there. No need to get upset. Get noticed through your excellent work. Become undeniably great. Remember—control your emotions. Don't let them control you.

If you're a man, why should you listen to women? Historically, it used to be the case that most industries were male-dominated. The man went to work and the woman stayed at home. It was very rare in the past to find women working at the same ratio as men. Men became very comfortable doing business with other men. In some industries, this is still the case, but this is changing and changing fast. A lot of women are entering the workforce with more dedication, commitment, and something to prove. With the increase in technology, a lot of women are now blessed with the ability to stay at home with their children and still run a business or be a key player in a business.

Business is a very masculine space. As more and more women enter this space, we can add a tremendous edge to a business because we see things differently. We see things in underserved markets, maybe markets that men have never thought about or could never access as a man. Women are also looking at things with a fresh pair of eyes, as we don't have all those years of old thinking and old ways. Our viewpoints are naturally more innovative. When women and men can really start to work together, that's when some of the greatest opportunities, products, and businesses will be created. We have to start to learn how to really work with one another rather than compete with one another. When this happens, it creates a culture of real strength and trust.

Women: Stop looking through the lens of what makes you feel good. "I am woman—hear me roar." No man wants to hear that stuff.

Men: Get over yourselves. You don't have all the answers. Start opening up to the possibility that someone who doesn't look like you could be the very thing that you need to take your business to the next level. Your greatest conversations aren't necessarily going to happen over cigars and cognac anymore. She might be in the middle of breastfeeding and have a moment of genius that she wants to share with you. I suggest you seriously start listening.

Start thinking like a businessPERSON.

What would a man do if he was overlooked? Men sometimes do get overlooked, too. They turn VIOLENT in their execution to make the people who overlooked them irrelevant. They create their OWN market. They give those people a middle finger and do not care one bit. They move on and fight harder for their vision. They start to see that *maybe I don't need you.* They test their convictions and take bolder actions. They Stand Alone.

All great people who have ever been on to something and have been shunned by others currently in higher places came back with a vengeance—not to sit at the table with these people but to create their own table! Some of the greatest people and stories in human history are about those who were once overlooked. Have you heard the name Anthony Michael Fadell? Anthony is an engineer and an inventor but really someone who could violently execute as an entrepreneur. He never gave up, despite the massive rejection he experienced from some of the biggest companies. He worked at Philips and pitched his product to them initially. No one could see what he was seeing. They didn't buy into his vision. He walked away from Philips and decided to work on this vision of his—his major problem was finding capital to fund his project.

Anthony withstood two years of rejection from some major companies with access to major capital to fund his innovative idea. They all said no—until he met someone different. He found another CEO and shared his product with him. At the time, this other CEO was also struggling. Tony continued to innovate and presented this prototype to the CEO. Let's just say that was the moment a dent in the universe was created. That CEO's name was Steve Jobs, and what Anthony had presented to him was the iPod. Anthony was put in charge of a new division within Apple and would go on to cofound the iPhone.

Who were those people that said no to Tony?

1. Philips
2. Microsoft
3. Palm
4. Nokia
5. Motorola
6. Blackberry

Anthony's ability to VIOLENTLY EXECUTE in the face of massive rejection, despite all the pushback, is what made him win and what makes him continue to win. There is a way, and you must carve it out by force. This is what all great people in business do. This is what I have done and continue to do.

After the creation of the iPod and iPhone, Anthony created another gadget company that wanted to make thermostats better. That small company is called Nest. Google acquired it from Anthony for 3.2 billion dollars.

I'm here to tell you that failure isn't the end. It could actually be the beginning if you learn to VIOLENTLY EXECUTE! You simply have to decide to Stand Alone.

CHAPTER 3

The Courage
It Takes To Win

THIS CHAPTER WILL examine the times we live in today. Instead of marching and chanting, we need to get to work. I'm grateful to be born in this time and place, when women have more rights than ever before. Is it perfect now? No. But it's a time to get inspired instead of offended.

I will provide an overview of how women can succeed in today's charged environment. I will also address men in business today. They are too soft, worried more about offending someone than doing great work. It's embarrassing when you are working with men and they are doing less and complaining and bitching more than anyone around them. That desire to hunt and provide for the family needs to be ignited for some men. I will show you—and them—how to enhance their performance to benefit everyone.

The world doesn't need more followers. We are living in a time where there is a call for leadership. What will it take for you to lead? It will take an enormous amount of courage. Every day that you are given life, all the decisions that you make are opportunities to fuel and feed your future self.

> *"Five percent of the people think. Ten percent think that they think, and the other eighty-five percent would rather die than think."*
>
> —*Thomas Edison*

Our thoughts and actions are inextricably connected. If you want to judge what a person is thinking about, look at their actions. We think we can trust a person's word, but I have learned from experience to watch how a person acts because it's a window into their thoughts, their principles, and what they value. And what a person thinks about is what they are surely creating for themselves.

So what are you doing to create a tougher, stronger, more powerful version of yourself?

If you look at your Instagram feed, is it filled with people feeding your mind with ideas that you are a victim, or is it filled with people fueling you with the power to take control of your own life and become a LEADER? The world today isn't designed to make you stronger. It's designed to make you weak so they can own you. The only people who are free from being owned are the people making the conscious decision to take the less traveled path, make the harder decision, and delay their instant gratification. There has never been a more difficult moment to do this. There is so much ease in this world, and it's killing our human spirit.

To be successful, you can't do what everyone is doing. You can't believe in what everyone is believing. You can't go where everyone else is going. It will take you being a leader in your life, making the decision to Stand Alone, and come to terms with what YOU are really capable of doing. This world is very noisy. Like a hum in a refrigerator, you don't realize it's going until someone pulls the plug. You instantly feel better. You feel lighter. There's less weighing you down. That hum is symbolic of the opinions and voices of everyone in your life. Those voices can start to become your voices if you don't start dictating another narrative.

You will have to think for yourself and grow your situational awareness. This is your ability to create your own rule book as you navigate in unknown territory and achieve what has never been done before. Sometimes you have to model someone else to get you to a certain place and then you have to be able to move on and do what has never been done before. You must first learn to disrupt YOURSELF.

There is a time to consume, and there is a time to create. I have done an enormous amount of reading in my life. I have studied war, what it takes, and the mindsets of leaders. Building the right instinct and not just knowing the right thing to do but the right TIME to do it is imperative for your success. If you make decisions, how do you navigate out of these errors and get yourself back on track? That's why we like watching movies. It's unbelievable how much someone can endure. Just when you think there is no way of them getting out of this, they do it again. They escape. Why do we like this? Because at one point or another, you will find yourself in a situation where you feel as though you are being backed into a corner and exactly what is inside of you will come out in these moments of your life. Tough situations don't make you—they reveal what's really inside of you. If you aren't training to be stronger and tougher every day, how will you be able to perform at your best level when it really counts?

Making a decision to do what is hard takes time, but it's necessary in order to overcome what is fast, easy, and feels good right away. What is right may even seem illogical and what is wrong may sound totally logical. You have to rise above the feeling and do what is right regardless of what it feels like. It's in that dark moment where you will be forced to Stand Alone. What will come out will be a reflection of what has been put in.

What are you putting in?

What are you training for?

What are you preparing yourself to handle in the future by the decisions you are making right now?

Most people are training a weaker version of themselves rather than a stronger version. That's why they quit so fast and often. Their spirit of "overcome and conquer" has been silenced by the spirit of getting offended. Inside of all of us is a victim and a conqueror. What you feed grows. Every time you do what is easy, you feed the victim. The victim always wants more ease. You start scanning your environment for the easy way to accomplish everything. As soon as it gets hard, you complain. The keyword for a victim is "fair."

Life isn't fair.

The most cruel things happen to the very best of us.

When you feed the conqueror inside of you, you deliberately choose to do what is right, not what is easy. You appear difficult and illogical to everyone else. That's why you have to be OK being alone. That's why you have to stop caring what everyone thinks about you and what they are saying.

Are you too sensitive as a person? Being too sensitive in business will make you go out of business. Being too sensitive in life will have you living a miserable life. Victims are easily offended. Being offended is not a new thing. It's just growing year by year. As life gets easier and easier, there is more to get offended by. How sensitive you are to an issue is an indication of what's inside of you. Think about when you have a small cut on your hand. How your body processes this cut will be determined by what's inside—the quality of your blood and your immune system. If you are healthy and you take good care of yourself, the wound heals. If you are unhealthy, a small cut can turn into a deadly infection. If you have an infection, this cut can immobilize you.

We become more sensitive the more infected we are with that victim mentality. The victim mentality is the lowest state to operate in. It's a diseased state. You will be offended by everything. Once you are offended, you start wasting precious energy; it snowballs, and more things start to offend you. Now you are distracted and not focused on achievement and creating. You have been immobilized.

Take a staph infection, for example, caused by members of the *Staphylococcus* genus of bacteria. These bacteria are everywhere. What matters is the state of your immune system, like any other infectious disease. A weak immune system will cause a staph infection to make everything so sensitive and inflamed that it will debilitate someone with a compromised immune system. The sensitivity will immobilize you.

What gets in and how we react is determined by what is INSIDE of us. Our world is made of trillions of microbes, viruses, and bacteria inside and outside of us. These trillions of microbes are like the noise of the world. They surround us all but only consume and take over the weak. Our body's immune system reads the information from these microbes and then creates a response depending on our state of health.

The mind is the same way. We take in the information of the world from so many places—our beliefs, the media, friends, family, etc. This information is processed by our minds. If we have done nothing to strengthen our minds, this negativity can consume us.

Remember the saying, "Sticks and stones can break my bones but words can never hurt me!" Whatever happened to that?

Words are handicapping people today, arresting their dreams, goals, and aspirations. Words can be like the staph infection that enters our system and gets into our bloodstream, and if your immune system isn't strong enough, you end up being overtaken by the enemy.

The enemy today may not be so obvious. In fact, it could be invisible, like a virus. A virus is simply a packet of information. A virus can kill someone with a weakened immune system or a person not optimized for a healthy life.

Our health isn't just on the outside and how we appear to people. Our health is also measured by our confidence, ambition, hunger, and drive to become more. If you are dormant and a virus or bacteria enters your body with more vigor to replicate, what do you think is going to happen?

That's why you need to care to grow. Make sure you thicken your skin.

The Navy SEALS that I have worked with talk about doing things that are hard and challenging so you can "callus" your mind. What is a callus? It literally means a thickening of your skin. After being exposed to friction or repetitive rubbing, a healthy immune response is created. A callus is formed as a function of the immune system to harden the skin and protect what is inside, usually a bone. Most of the time, the tissue is void of nerves, so it becomes desensitized to the pressure and irritation of the external environment.

DESENSITIZE YOURSELF. Learn how to withstand enormous amounts of pressure and friction. Now you can see the genius behind the statement of forming a callus on your mind.

Here's the thing: Humans are both complex and simple. We are not just our physical bodies. We are also spiritual. It's not as easy to measure our spiritual data, but we see this in people every day. Their hunger, their drive, that unbelievable ability to overcome despite enormous odds stacked up against them.

Being successful will make you desensitized for a period of time, where you have to be able to ignore the noise of the world to maintain your focus and stay on task. But to Stand Alone means you take it to a whole new level. You understand that you cannot remain desensitized. You have to understand where the other side is coming from, and through understanding, you can make an even greater impact. Have situational awareness. See the bigger picture. Remember what it feels like to be in these bad places so you don't do it to someone else to cause them unnecessary and intentional harm.

> *Show me the boy before the age of seven, and I will show you the man that they will become.*

I was called a tiger when I was younger. I was known for sitting quietly and watching.

I have always loved to observe. I talk for a living, but I take in enormous amounts of data through learning by reading and observing. I run this data through my own challenges in life. That's called experience. The harder the experience, the better.

For most people living in North America, the issue is that you really haven't been through that much when you compare it to someone living on the other side of the planet. That's where the immigrant advantage comes into play. We all know the saying, "Never bet against an immigrant." The reason is that they endured far more than most of us could imagine. Their training was tougher. So when it's time to perform, they are more prepared because of what they have already been through. That's why you never curse a bad experience. It can and will make you better if you allow it to.

At twenty-four years old, I decided to move to the States. Being twenty-four years old in 2005 was an advantage. How and when you were raised matters. Our environment shapes us. Do you have the courage to place yourself intentionally in an environment that will break you so you can be rebuilt stronger?

What did you grow up seeing? Who did you grow up with? Who were you being programmed by? Those first years of life, what were you taking in as normal?

My normal was not normal. I'm so happy I never had a brother to compete with. My father raised his daughters like we were the sons he never had. There were no princess moments. I didn't compete in beauty pageants—I competed in math and science competitions. I didn't have a pink room and a princess bed with Barbies all around. No one was making us breakfast in bed and serving us. We were doing the serving.

The decline of generations is a very real thing, partially because some people get soft after a hard experience. They want to give their children everything they couldn't have, so they end up spoiling their children. Look and listen to that word: SPOIL. You ruin your children when you give them everything instead of cultivating them into people who can achieve greatness on their own. That's why so many people have such big self-esteem issues today. Suicide rates are increasing because of a lack of confidence.

There are real self-esteem issues today. Self-esteem is the esteem that only we can give to ourselves. SELF-esteem. Most people today think this is something we get from other people. We build our self-esteem by doing hard things and overcoming obstacles. The more help we are given, the less self-esteem we will have.

That's why hard times create strong men and good times create weak men.

Proverbs 13:24

Whoever spares the rod hates their children, but the one who loves their children is careful to discipline them.

Confidence comes from doing something on your own. Being productive and doing your own work with excellence is what builds confidence. Confidence comes from learning and growing through hard and challenging times. In these times, we develop skills and attributes like courage and faith—putting these skills and attributes inside of you serves you—rather than filling yourself with excuses and becoming a victim of this world.

Giving a child everything creates an entitled individual, but creating an environment that allows them to stretch their wings and exercise their capacity to do things on their own—and do them well—creates a future leader.

Most parents today fail to discipline their children, and the workforce is paying heavily for it. We see this when we approach someone in a service position and they can barely muster the energy to greet you properly. They give you the feeling that you are bothering them rather than greeting you with a smile and going above and beyond in service to perform excellent work and do everything in their power to earn your business. These are the same people who end up marching for increased wages and wonder why robots are coming to replace them.

Instead of thinking, "What can I get?" think, "What can I give?" Many people don't think like that because they weren't raised to serve. They were being served as they were raised. That's the difference.

When my father was waking up in the morning, I had to make him coffee and breakfast. I was being programmed to know that he was going to work, so that meant that we had to go to work, too. We were servants in our house. If there was a dish in the sink when he came home, we would hear about it.

This is why I have no problem serving today. I understand the importance of SERVICE. A person growing up in a world where everything is done for them becomes an entirely different person than one who grows up and has to do everything for themselves and everyone else.

Today there are child labor laws that protect children. That's another North American thing. No one in the East thinks that children shouldn't be contributing to the family's bottom line.

I am aware that my children are growing up in a world entirely different from the one I grew up in. I know I must do everything in my power to install these values into them. They are constantly being taught to serve. As a parent today, I am constantly thinking about what more I can make our children do. How can I create an environment that allows them to contribute rather than just consume?

I grew up cutting my father's nails. Think about that. Visualize what it means to cut someone's nails. If you have ever cut a baby's nails, you will understand the delicateness behind it. In the act of serving someone, you realize that there is a relationship there. As strong and as tough as my father was, there was a bond that was being created. I was learning the art of taking care of someone. I was subconsciously learning how to take care of someone who is taking care of me.

When my father kicked me out on my own at the age of nineteen, it was the right thing to do. I had broken the bond that was created. I was forced into one of the darkest times of my life. Alone. Now, I had to learn to lead and take care of myself. That's what I had to do to create my own self. What emerged was an even greater version of myself— when I could truly see what I was capable of doing on my own.

You will never be what you are supposed to become living under the rule of your parents. The Bible talks about leaving your father's house:

In the Old Testament Abraham was called by God (Genesis 12: 1-3):

The LORD had said to Abram, "Go from your coun-try, your people and your father's household to the land I will show you.

"I will make you into a great nation, and I will bless you; I will make your name great, and you will be a blessing.

I will bless those who bless you, and whoever curses you I will curse; and all peoples on earth will be blessed through you."

I was being called. You, too, are being called. You must leave your father's house. Your children will prosper if you continue to have the courage to lead them right. Your business and life will only prosper if you have the courage to lead it, not just live in it.

What happens to us is really happening *for* us. When my father cut my wings at the age of nineteen, it was an opportunity to regrow my wings even stronger, like an eagle that reaches its vulnerable age where it must make a decision to die or re-grow its talons, its beak, and shed the dead weight of old feathers. The eagle's rebirth is a reminder that it will be painful to regrow, but the alternative is death, so we don't really have a choice. There are moments in your life where you have to be led by your decision to always move forward and com-pletely disassociate from the alternative of falling back, quitting, or running away. Choose life. Always choose life—no matter how pain-ful it is. Life and forward movement is always the right answer. Suffer and grow back stronger by choosing to endure and move forward.

How does the eagle know to do this? There is no manual for the eagle to read on how to live, how to adapt, and grow—it must learn through watching its elders. It has instinct to lead it and tell it what it should do. What is your instinct? I'm grateful that my parents are not quitters. Having suffered the loss of their first child after moving to a brand new country, they made a decision to forge ahead. While my father was as tough as they come with us, it planted a seed inside of me that I too would also be able to endure and that hard times would never break me but instead would provide an opportunity for me to have a period of rebirth and transformation.

Being forced to fend for myself and pay my way through five years of university with no assistance and work a full time job doing multiple shifts—sometimes not sleeping because I had to stay up and study—would cultivate MY work ethic. The same thing I witnessed in my father working three jobs at the same time and not sleeping was a seed of instinct that was planted in me. Instead of retracting, I moved ahead.

After university, when I made a decision to move to the United States, it was another period of rebirth. I would have to pluck the feathers of wanting to become a doctor to learn how to sell and run a professional business. It wasn't easy, but I always knew that if I worked harder at the task and kept my mind away from the current circumstance, I would make it through.

My parents made it the best that they knew how, and it provided a foundation for me to make it. People always ask me what drives me. It's hard to articulate it into words sometimes because it feels like something much larger than just a goal or a vision that I have. It really does feel like something coming from within me. My parents never spoke about their first born that passed away. No one in my family really did. It was something that we knew so little about. I always wondered why that was. When you think of the eagle plucking away its old feathers so that it wouldn't weigh it down as it continues to fly, the feathers become symbolic of the events in our past.

We are not eagles. We are far more than any animal that God has ever created. We were created in His image. We can learn from nature and apply its lessons and instincts to our lives to live at a higher level. While the eagle knew it had to go through the painful process of removing the old weighted feathers, those feathers were discarded. I believe that we are able to take this example to a whole different level.

As you grow older, you start to realize that nothing is ever really lost. This goes back to the law of energy: Energy cannot be created or destroyed—it just transfers from one form to another. Every single experience is never lost; it should never be discarded. We can put it aside, but it will always come back to serve us if we allow it or destroy us if we don't confront the lesson. My relationship with my parents at the time when they let me go felt like there was no coming back to them. It was over. It was so painful. It wasn't until I had children that I really understood what they would have gone through losing their first child. It made me have so much respect for them. I always felt a connection to my older sister whom I never met. It's as though I live so large to live for the both of us. I remember that she never got a chance to live out her dreams, and that's why I never take for granted any opportunity that I receive. I'm grateful for it all. Each day that I am gifted life means the world to me. I don't want to play small. I want to live for more than just myself.

When my little girl Sophia turned two years old, I had to leave to go to the airport for a business trip. As I was leaving, she was holding my suitcase, and she said, "Where's Cindy?" Cindy was the name of my older sister who passed away. Cindy passed away when she was two years old. My daughter, when she turned two years old, was asking for her? It was a moment that confirmed to me that nothing is ever lost, and everything—good and bad—can be used to grow a better future if we allow it.

> *"What gets us into trouble is not what we don't know. It's what we know for sure that just ain't so."*
>
> —*Mark Twain*

Today's ideology of an independent woman is very misleading to young females. One of the most important decisions that you will ever make is who you decide to marry. Often when you are young, you make this decision out of convenience, and you get wrapped into relationships that don't end up serving you but instead end up hurting you tremendously. If there is any advice that I would offer to our children—especially our daughter—it's to make sure she doesn't marry anyone until she knows who she is. And that definitely isn't until after twenty-five years old. Why do I say twenty-five? That's the age where the decision part of our brain—the prefrontal cortex—matures. This is the part of the brain that is designated to executive function. It helps us to make decisions and problem solve through reasoning and comprehension. It's also the part of the brain that moderates impulse control and perseverance. I can't think of two more important traits to pick a proper partner than impulse control and perseverance! Before this part of the brain is matured, we can really make stupid decisions.

The people in our lives who we are around the most have the greatest impact in our lives and who we become. Choose wisely.

Most women today are being raised in an environment and a world that speaks about being "strong" and "independent." The truth is, learning how to work with your partner is key to your success. You can do more together than you can do apart. We are not operating in a closed system. Our environment shapes us. If you study energy, you understand that it doesn't get created or destroyed; it just transfers from one form to another. This is true for life. This is how our experiences work. We think we are creating an experience, but really our past is creating our future. You can't destroy what has happened to you. But you can USE it to make a better future. You have to take what has happened and let it TRANSFORM you. Nothing goes away. Inside all of it is an infinite library, books and words of what we can do and what we can become. Our genes are not determining what we will do. In the same way, a book cannot change you unless you open the book up, start reading, and execute on it.

Our DNA is the same way: Our environment controls what gets expressed in our DNA. This is epigenetics. What we are around triggers the expression of our DNA. It's not the DNA that makes us— it's what gets expressed that matters. We are all being triggered by our environment. Who are the people that we choose to surround ourselves with that we ALLOW to share our environment and ultimately shape us is a powerful force in our lives. Who we choose to surround ourselves with literally builds or destroys us.

I don't think there is anything that can have a greater impact in your life than who you choose to marry. How many dreams have been destroyed because of a spouse? However true, this person can also become your greatest source of strength and power.

I think a lot of women are put in a very uncomfortable situation today where we want to express ourselves as strong and independent. I have always known that independence doesn't really exist from my studies in science, and we must come to terms with the fact that the people who we choose to have in our lives absolutely do have an effect on us. We can't be isolated and alone if we want to be successful. We have to learn to work with the right people. Like the eagle's feathers, maybe it's time to do some plucking. This is incredibly hard to do. Remember that no relationship is ever lost. Let the time you had together serve you and remember that some relationships need a pause button. I know if I was around all the people of my past, I wouldn't have achieved as much as I have. I am constantly examining this for myself.

This is especially true for business teams. Business is not for the faint of heart. There will be people who you start with who won't finish with you, and that's OK.

A business is made up of people and different departments (often with very different personality types). It's why I like calling my business an organization—it has to be highly organized to be functional. There are a lot of parts that work separately and connect to everything at the same time. It sounds confusing because it is. Just like how we all want to be free and be our own boss—the only problem with that is that we all have a boss. Above and below. People who can put us out of work if we fail to perform. That could be a customer or a shareholder—it doesn't need to be someone with a corner office and a title, although those exist too.

To be successful in business, we have to get all the parts working together in a functional system. When you are dealing with people, this is often a very challenging thing to do.

We have people in our business, colleagues and associates who become like family members who could be creating a hinderance, but because they are familiar, it's hard to cleave. Sometimes it gets difficult holding them accountable because we are too emotionally entangled with them. They were with us when we had no one, and now we know better, we see farther—and they don't. What do you do?

Without a deep level of trust, doing great business becomes impossible. This trust has to come from both sides. Trust comes from having character AND competence. Being a good person isn't enough. If you are a good person but you are terrible at your job, it will damage the business. Look at people and ask yourself if they care to get better. Are they working on developing their skills, or are they just complacent and coasting along? Do they take the initiative to learn more—to do more? Or are they just doing enough? Competence is required, and incompetence is a disease. Some people are competent to a certain level, and you can never promote someone higher than the level to which they are willing to develop themselves. I see this happen a lot. People get a title or a position and grow into it by getting better.

This takes time and patience, and it's worth it if they are doing the work. It's a complete disaster if they aren't doing the work and expect for everything to just fall into place for themselves.

We can also have a situation in business where a team member can be very competent, but they have some serious character flaws. This is the worst case scenario because these people will always think they are protected because they can get the job done. But are they really getting the job done if they are not doing it with character and integrity? A great business cares *how* you get the job done. You have to have a moral compass. You have to operate within the confines of the regulations of the company and the industry that you are in. Just like sports—you have to play within the boundaries of the field, or you are no longer playing that game. Get some morals and ethics. Do what's right all the time. Have a "do whatever it takes" mentality, and make sure whatever it takes is legal and ethical. Business people today need character training. How you handle power is a product of the character you possess. I learned about power dynamics before I got into leadership roles so that I would see what happens to people and why. Reading business biographies from very successful business people is incredibly important because it will help guide you and make you understand that all people are placed in moments where they have to make character calls. You don't want to drop the ball here. The damage that it will create is too great to measure.

Character and competence creates culture. The culture of the organization is what it accepts from others. When this is low, your company culture will suffer. When this is high, the company will thrive. It will be an environment where more is expected with the standard of excellence.

We all bring insecurities into the relationships that we have. That's what makes relationships so hard. If there isn't that deep trust that is established and maintained, it gets *really* hard to be real in a relationship, and then you run the risk of not feeling fulfilled. It takes a lot of work to make relationships work, but having real relationships has been the greatest and most rewarding experience for me.

Remember that nothing is lost. We follow ourselves everywhere we go. The real person who we have to know and understand is ourselves. When we do this, we become clear about who we want to have around us. Finding the right people who you can grow WITH—that means you are growing and they are growing—is also the key. When we can find people who want to grow as much as we want or are willing to support our growth and not do anything to destroy it, we have tapped into something magnificent. The world is filled with quitters. It's just so much easier for people to walk away. That's why people do it—because it's easier. They walk away from opportunities that get challenging. They walk away from relationships that challenge them. Instead, what you need to be able to do is find the courage to stay a little longer. Find the courage to see what is happening to create the circumstance that you are in. Find YOUR responsibility in your current circumstance and then find the courage to respond rather than react. Quitting is a reaction. Endurance and understanding take tremendous discipline. Can you find the strength to do what very few are willing to do? Is it possible to work through the pain and get to the other side where there could be a tremendous amount of pleasure? Stand Alone and feed your courage to do what's right.

A Psalm of David (Psalm 23, ESV)
The LORD is my shepherd;
I shall not want.

He makes me lie down in green pastures.
He leads me beside still waters.

He restores my soul.

He leads me in paths of righteousness
For His name's sake.

Even though I walk through the valley of the shadow
of death,
I will fear no evil,
For You are with me;
Your rod and Your staff, they comfort me.

You prepare a table before me in the presence of my enemies;
You anoint my head with oil;
My cup overflows.

Surely goodness and mercy shall follow me
All the days of my life,
And I shall dwell in the house of the LORD forever.

NIV
Even though I walk
through the darkest valley,
I will fear no evil,
for you are with me.

So going back to this independent women issue—strong men are not the problem. Weak men are. It takes a really strong man to work with strong women, and it takes a mature and wise woman to understand that strong doesn't mean being all by yourself. To have a healthy relationship, it will take you pursuing strong men and having respectful relationships with them in order to succeed at a higher level. It will take you constantly working on yourself to grow in your wisdom and understanding that we can't do anything great by ourselves. It will take us being our best and working with others who care to be their best as well.

There has never been a greater call for strong leadership. The leader who has the courage to stand up against weakness. The leader who doesn't care about not offending but still doesn't want to offend. They do what's right all the time. If they make mistakes, they own up to it instead of hiding it because they understand that nothing is ever lost and what we suppress will come out in another form some other way. It's better to deal with whatever issues you are going through than run away and hide from facing the reality of the situation. Strong leaders will understand human nature. But they will be guided by higher standards rather than the acceptable norm. They will learn to control their emotions and lead by example to create a culture that can produce other strong leaders.

CHAPTER 4

Learn the Rules of the Game and Play to WIN

W HAT IS FAMILIAR to you?

People who endure hardships are preparing themselves to handle more in the future. The point of life is not to live with ease. If we give everything to a child, how are they prepared to handle difficulty in their future? Our power is in our preparation.

I see this a lot. I have a ton of young want-to-be-entrepreneurs that come into the business thinking they can do whatever they want and be whatever they want. Then business smacks them straight in the face, punches them in the gut, and forces them to fall flat on their face. They are in complete and utter shock. Then they start murmuring and complaining that this isn't for them. What isn't for you?

This is business. This is life. It's not a smooth ride. There are a ton of potholes, and you might fall off the cliff if you don't know what you are doing. Coming into any situation blind and unprepared is never a good thing. That's why many start in business but so few will finish.

The point of life is to learn the rules of the game and play it to WIN. Winning is something that sounds really great. If you have ever experienced a win in your life, you felt like you were on a cloud when you were being acknowledged and celebrated. But you know what it really takes. You know that to get to that cloud you had to go through things that most are not willing to endure.

So many people today are too focused on making things easier. As parents, when we ourselves were raised tough, we instead want to over-love our children. In the Bible it says that "perfect love casts out fear" (*1 John 4:18, ESV*)—*perfect* love. A love that has the courage to correct and not care what people think but care more about what they are becoming. If we went through something challenging, it's normal to want to make sure no one ever goes through those same challenges. But what does that really do to a person? Instead of helping, we actually hurt people when we don't allow them the space and time needed to navigate through the hardships of their life.

Hardships create heroes. God doesn't bless us by making our lives void of challenges or difficulties. He loves us *perfectly* and that means he brings opportunities for us to grow and develop ourselves. These opportunities come in the form of the challenges we continuously face so we must face them head on without fear. People are inspired by stories of people overcoming hardships and winning because it shows us that we can do it, too. What you don't want is someone doing it for you. The more someone does for you, the more your courage dies inside of you. Courage is a muscle that grows with repeated use. Excellence requires repetition. The more we learn to endure through hardships, the easier it gets. Then, what used to be hard becomes easy.

To win in this game of life, you must first know what game you're playing. If I'm playing chess, I have to know all the pieces on the board. What each piece can and cannot do. The game already has established rules. Imagine playing chess like you are playing checkers. You will look like a fool. You don't stand a chance to win.

If I want to teach my child how to play chess, he first has to know all the pieces and what each piece can do. This is not the time to use his imagination and express himself. Why? Because if he wants to play with other people, he must learn the rules. You must be willing to discipline yourself and give yourself order and structure first so you have a base to be able to interact with one another. Once a base is established, then you can start to differentiate from the other players. But if you try to stand out too prematurely, you will end up hurting yourself more than helping yourself.

When we are teenagers, we all want to stand out. As we get older, we look at all the foolish things we did with embarrassment. We did those things because we didn't really know who we were. Go tell a teenager they don't know who they are and see what happens to you. There is so much more to learn about life. There is so much this child will have to live through to learn how things really work. Letting children do what they want prematurely is the quickest path to their destruction.

As we age, we become clearer, and we make decisions from a stronger foundation. You have made all the errors. You have grown through them and are stronger. You learned the rules of the game. You learned how things really work. This must happen before you can play to win.

Confusion is the enemy of execution.

Most people don't make it in business because they don't know the rules. Work brings order and structure into our lives. It's something that we have to be in good relationship with.

How were you raised to view work? Did you have a parent who didn't work? Is that familiar to you? Did you have a stay-at-home mom? Is that familiar to you? How do you navigate in a world that demands so much from you as a parent, as a spouse, AND as a provider? It's not easy. What I will say is that it's never been easier to manage. As a business owner and CEO of a company, I never thought I would want to be at home. The truth is I don't all the time, but I love having this option. I absolutely love cooking, baking, being at home with the children, and watching them grow. I know I won't have this season with them forever, and I am so appreciative of being able to run a company and take it all in. I worked my butt off when I had no kids. I see young people wasting time when they have so little to be responsible for. You can't do this. Pay the price early or you will pay the price later on. All those trips and vacations I didn't take, all those weekends I worked while other people were partying or having a good time were like an investment that built with compound interest for my future. I'm able to pay for a private teacher, private school, homeschool the children if needed, and be in charge of what they are learning and give them an educational boost when they are young. I'm able to work efficiently from home if I choose to our bring the kids to the office with me. When I travel, I can bring them with me if I choose. All these options were created ahead of time.

Early in my career, I was rigid. I was about total structure and order, and this is what created the freedoms for me later on. I was able to sacrifice early on because of what I wanted in the future—the freedom to choose.

My mother worked intensely. She was supposed to be a medical doctor, and I believe that moving to a different country with a new family sent her in a different direction. They say that a girl will treat herself the way that her mother treats herself. I think this is true. My mother is a quiet woman. Her mother was an even more quiet woman. I watched my mother be strong in her own ways. She never complained. For all that she endured, she took everything in great stride.

My parents lost their firstborn right after they came to Canada. I was supposed to have another sister. She died when she was two years old. My parents had just moved from a country in South America to a town in Ontario, Canada. I can't even begin to imagine what parents go through when they suffer the loss of a child. The natural order sometimes gets disrupted in life.

This is how business is. We are doing everything right, and then for some unexplained reason, a massive disaster strikes. We find ourselves lost in the chaos and disorder of the moment. We have an option at that moment: We can stop, or we can keep going.

You must always keep going. Keep moving forward.

I'm so glad my parents kept going and decided to have more children rather than be engulfed in that tragedy. I often think about what strain the death of a child could put on a relationship. It's truly unbelievable that they were able to move through this together. It probably felt like hell on earth to them.

My parents' education also wasn't recognized in Canada, so they had to start all over with that. For my mom, she went from studying to be a doctor to working as a microbiologist. She gave birth to three more girls in a span of five years. I have a sister who is two years older than me and a younger sister who is three years younger than me. Yes, I'm a middle child. And yes, everything they say about middle children is true!

My parents did the absolute best with what they had. My mom is someone I have so much respect and honor for. I don't have a super close relationship with my mother the way I see in most North American mother and daughter relationships, but this doesn't change the way I feel about her. Every mother goes through the pains of weighing work with raising a family. For my mother, there wasn't an option.

Both my parents had to work to survive in their new country. My father had to work security jobs while studying to advance himself so he could work as a lab technician. My mother always worked in downtown Toronto, while my father worked in the suburbs of Toronto. Having two cars was a luxury for my parents. When my mother finally got her first car, I remember being so embarrassed when we would drive by kids we knew that I would duck and hide. When it rained, the water leaked into the car, and we had a bucket that we used to scoop the water out so we could sit in it and not damage our shoes. At one point, the starter didn't work, so I remember that my mom had to hit the middle console with a hammer to get it to start. Sounds too crazy to be true, right? Trust me—it was.

I remember traveling to work with my mother one time and her driving over an hour to park and catch the train for another hour to get downtown. It took us over three hours of traveling that day, almost two hours to get home that evening. All to then become a wife and mother as soon as she stepped in the door. Most mornings, my mom would cook a meal before she left to go to work. I would get mad at her because she made the house smell like food, and I hated smelling like the food at school. Welcome to the life of living in a home with immigrant parents. There was no Grubhub or DoorDash. Our parents struggled to make ends meet and never wanted us eating "outside food."

Cooking, cleaning, laundry, traveling three to four hours a day to get to work, working in a job where you dumb yourself down because of life's circumstances, dealing with the loss of your first daughter and dealing with three living daughters, dealing with a husband who wasn't exactly a walk in the park...I honestly can't imagine what life was like for my mother in her mind.

Maybe that's why so many women in the past were so silent; because if the dam broke, it would be like the water breaking in childbirth—all hell breaking loose. I'm grateful that I can express myself in ways that my mother would never have been able to. But I still think every woman (including myself) is silently dealing with something else. When we portray that we are strong, we sometimes are masking other areas in our life where we are falling apart. We look like we have it all figured out, and the truth is we are still learning like everyone else.

Just like my parents coming to Canada, I came to the USA with a car and a bag of clothes. I built everything from the ground up. The opportunities for growth and wealth had never been better, so it was the right time to make the move. I slept on the floor, and I now sleep in the most luxurious places. There is a time and place for everything.

What you are going through you have to GROW THROUGH. In order to do this, you have to learn the rules of the game and you MUST play to win!

Standing Alone is about doing what it takes to succeed regardless of how uncomfortable it feels. When you put yourself all out there, you will feel very uncomfortable. Something has to be lost. In order to keep growing and advancing, you need to be able to Stand Alone.

I can't think of another animal that gets this better than the hermit crab. We are all like hermit crabs in the pandemic of 2020. A hermit is a person who lives in solitude. A hermit crab without a shell is a death sentence. They will be cooked in the sun on land and stung or eaten in the water. They live in dependence on something else because of their soft tails. The tail of the hermit crab never gets exposed. It stays soft, unlike the other body parts that are exposed to the elements and harden with time and exposure.

Like an arm kept in a cast, it atrophies and becomes weak. We become weak every time we fail to expose ourselves to a challenge, a new opportunity, or a new chance to grow. Growth can't happen without exposure. Exposure is dangerous and feels unsafe—that's why most don't do it.

When the hermit crab starts to outgrow its borrowed shell of protection, it needs to find another one that will be bigger—but not so big that it can no longer be mobile. In fact, if there are multiple hermit crabs, they will line up in order from smallest to largest to make sure that each person has the right fit.

That doesn't mean things always go smoothly. Just like in business, you need to be respectful of a natural order. I've seen so many people who don't want to grow into their borrowed shell. Instead, they want the biggest right away. Getting the biggest doesn't help you—it can hurt you. You can get promoted to a level of incompetence. You don't start a business and get the biggest office and then decide to start filling it up. That will eat away at your profits. It sucks you dry from being creative and putting the money into use in other areas that could help the business perform better. Many smaller deals practiced diligently in the beginning prepare us for the bigger deals later on that we can execute with excellence.

But there absolutely does come a time where we outgrow our shell. Staying in too small of a space can be suffocating. As living and breathing organisms, we all take cues from our outside world. The crab has tentacles and feelers to check out a shell to see if it will be a right fit.

You have to build your intuition. Maybe you are in a company right now where you are not the boss, but you are learning from a really good boss. Learn as much as you can, no matter where you are. This is how you make an investment into your future. If all you do is just enough, you can't get ahead. You don't have to ask for a raise. You have to do more than you are currently being paid for, and that's how you become more valuable to the organization.

There will come a time when you outgrow that shell and need a new shell. That will be a phase of great vulnerability. Your weakest areas will become exposed, and it could cost you everything. These are the trade-offs that we make for growth.

Growth doesn't happen by itself. There is someone or something applying a force to a system that creates that growth. By itself, entropy increases. Do nothing, and disorder will appear. Growth is a by-product of putting EXTRA work into a system for the desired outcome.

This is why you never have to compete with anyone. Comparing yourself to where someone else is on their journey is like a small hermit crab envying a larger shell. You have to grow into your shell. When you outgrow it, you have to be able to pursue new and better opportunities that you can grow into. The larger shell may do even more damage to you depending on where you are in your growth cycle.

Business works and functions in cycles. Look at all life processes. Everything has a beginning and an end. Your needs will not be the same as someone who is in a different part of the cycle.

When you start in business, everything is new. It's like a child. They are paying attention to everything because everything is new. This is where a lot of people get very distracted and end up falling off the cliff. You're training, it's hard, nothing really makes sense. You keep getting told to trust the process, and you really have to do that. In each part of the cycle, you have to Stand Alone.

If you are paying too much attention to people who are in a similar situation to you, you will end up in further trouble. It's like people complaining in a boat that's about to descend into the falls. You need help from an outside source to rescue you. Panicking in the boat will just make things worse.

This is why mentors are so great in business. What you are panicking about, someone else has already been through. This is why the ideal thing is to work with people at a higher level than you so they can help guide you. For a lot of women getting into business, this means you have to be familiar with working with strong men. I say strong men because you need to stay the heck away from weak men. Weak men have manipulated their way into their position and will misguide you or have you doing something you don't want to be doing.

I have seen this happen in business. Men have been training to do battle in the boardroom. They can go at one another and have lunch right after. I've also seen them cut off people high and dry to suffocate their competition. Do not be naive. Not all people are there to help you. Another thing about weak people in business is that they are not creative, but if they have a big ego to feed, they will steal all your ideas and give you zero credit for them.

You shouldn't share all your ideas with everyone. It's important that you build partnerships with people you can trust and with people who have a vested interest in your success. And especially with people who have shared values and a shared mission and purpose. When you can align with the right people in business, you will go way farther than you can get on your own.

Be careful about people with titles and no skills; these are the most dangerous. They are the super-spreaders of your ideas and will diminish all the hard work that you put in to separate yourself from the pack.

Make no mistake about it: You win in business by doing more than everyone else, by doing it better than everyone else, and by doing it longer than everyone else. The best is when you can get all three working for you, but if you are just doing enough, never going the extra mile, doing sub-par work, and quitting prematurely, it isn't going to work for you. That's why you have to make yourself familiar with being uncomfortable and stay with a problem long enough to find the solution.

A lot of people like the idea of being a serial entrepreneur, investing in many businesses. But that only happens once you have achieved a level of mastery at something specific. Have you mastered selling? Have you mastered the art of presenting? Have you mastered the ability to close, negotiate, influence? Have you mastered the art of working and getting the right people on your team and working with them?

The future of workplaces won't excel because its members have a variety of skin colors and genders. They will excel because their teams will bring forth a variety of skills that complement one another, and, when integrated as a team, they become unstoppable.

There is also a big void of women in leadership positions that companies would stand to benefit tremendously from if they learned how to work with strong females. This will require parents to have the courage to raise strong females. And men who are in the current leadership positions must take the responsibility to not get intimidated by working with strong females, but welcome it.

I will never forget the men who believed in me and invested in my success on my professional journey. Don't worry, I had my fair share of men who were terrible to me, also. But all it took was for a handful to see something more. We will all have PEOPLE who are good and bad to us. Do your best as you are learning to stop labeling people with words like "all" and "everyone." "All men are…" "All women are this…" "Everyone is…" When someone does something to hurt us, the first thing that we want to do is to make sense of it. Why are they doing this? Our brain is a pattern-making machine. This serves us and can also hurt us. We must learn to lead our brain. We start to label and stereotype if we don't. Seeing patterns is a design in our brain to help us be more energy efficient. Pattern recognition is what can give you an edge, and it can also help you anticipate what will happen. Our brain takes in millions of bits of information per second.

Millions. Think about that—if we processed every little thing we saw, we would never have the energy to do anything. The brain is energy expensive, so it has developed mechanisms to filter through all this information and point out what is important for you to see to keep you alive. That's why your brain is naturally negative. It amplifies and points out what is wrong so you can "pay" attention to it in case this thing is trying to kill you. We "pay" attention. What we focus on costs us. When you Stand Alone, you start to pay attention to the things that really matter, not the things that we are driven to by default. When we don't put effort into focusing where our attention goes, it ends up costing us our best version of ourselves because we are wasting energy on what is not important.

When I came into business, I was so young and naive. I had zero understanding of what the business world was like. My background for my entire life was in science as I was studying to be a doctor. The benefit of this was it helped me to understand systems and processes and how things work. I applied this understanding to business and was able to see a bigger picture that helped me to become a leader with ownership rather than just a worker.

In university, I had the opportunity to extend my studies for one more year and graduate with two majors. My first major was life sciences (biology and chemistry), and I decided to do my second major in religion. Little did I know how much this was going to help me in understanding and working with people. I took a powerful course in humanities that had me study some great injustices in the world.

What I can say about learning about the greatest injustices that have taken place throughout history is that the first person you have to save is yourself. Being unemployed, living off your parents, and tweeting about social injustices does very little to help the world. If you want to save the dolphins or save Darfur, you must first save yourself.

I am so grateful that I had to learn the hard way to pay for everything for myself so that I didn't have the time or money to get wrapped up in other people's messes. I worked full-time and went to school full-time. Any spare time that I had was spent either picking up extra shifts to make more money or studying for my exams. I still have nightmares sometimes about not finishing all my course requirements and not being able to graduate because I missed my classes. It was a lot to juggle.

When I would hear about other families going to events and on vacations, I knew this wasn't an option for me. This trained a work ethic in me like no one else. But again, this also had always been very familiar to me. My mom worked as hard as she did, and my father worked three shifts to make ends meet. He would leave the house at 7:00 a.m. for his first job at the main hospital where he worked, and then he would do extra hours at a private lab from 4:00 p.m. to midnight. He picked up another shift from midnight until 8:00 a.m. in the morning at another hospital.

While most parents today are trying to have work/life balance, I know this is the greatest myth of life. There was no balance for my parents, and I had ZERO balance while I was in school and working full-time. I was familiar with an extremely great work ethic. It's something I hope to pass on to our children; I hope to never get comfortable and complacent but to push the limits of what I am capable of achieving so that they can do the same for themselves and their families. I have received the greatest inheritance from my parents. I inherited all the great qualities to win in this world—and to me, that's better than money.

Today, people are doing everything to disrupt order, hierarchies, and chains of command. It won't end well. There is a natural order to things that we have to learn to respect.

I don't just respect this, I admire it.

Have order in your home, business, and life. Do first things first. Imagine that the hermit crabs can line up in an orderly fashion from biggest to smallest to fit into appropriate shells—and humans are loitering, stealing, trying to take what is theirs to recover from the sins of the past.

In the business world, there are the business elites. It will always be that way. But you have to take refuge in understanding that there has never been a better time to get in the game, and you must want to play to win. It isn't about everyone winning—it's about the best of the best winning.

Mention the word pyramid in business and people will get nervous. Can you please tell me what a pyramid is? Our school system is a pyramid. Healthcare is a pyramid. The flow of money and the distribution of wealth is in the shape of a pyramid. That's because many start and very few finish. That's what creates the pyramid. If everyone kept going, applied themselves, and kept learning, more would be able to get to the top.

In my insurance business, I am the only woman who has made it to the very top. The year I won every imaginable award with my team, some people in the company did everything in their power to pull me down from the top. It's a constant battle when people don't understand you. Or even worse, misunderstand you.

What you have to do is make sure YOU understand YOU. Have the courage to Stand Alone and keep playing the game to win. Have the courage to stop competing with people because you aren't even in the same game anymore. When you learn to Stand Alone, you are creating a lane for yourself; You start running your race, and you no longer spend energy and attention wondering what others are doing or thinking about you. This is when you can truly dominate.

In the next chapter, I will break this down in detail with the Seven Rules for Dominating.

But first, let me leave you with this: You will never experience freedom without first having order, structure, and discipline in your life. To move from disorder to order takes force. The natural order of things is entropy. Entropy states that disorder is more likely to occur than order. Things get messy before they get better because of entropy. As you expand, order gets less likely and randomness increases.

That's why systems are important. But you have to make sure that you are always leading the system or you can run the risk of lowering creativity and innovation. Never get too systematic and slow. A lot of corporations do this in the form of red tape, consistently saying no, and bureaucracy. This will kill a company. We saw this happen with Blockbuster, Kodak, and K-mart (we will cover this more in detail in Chapter 10).

There is a time where you are going to be vulnerable. You will have to expose yourself to the open air and waters, to other people. There are times when you will need to be under the shell, under the tutelage of someone else. But then there comes a time to grow. To move to the other shell. Exit the cage and go into a roomier cage that you can grow into. Timing and sequence matters. Be willing to trust the guidance of others whenever you are first learning anything new. We have to be coachable. A skeptic mind can't take anything in. After you master the basics from great coaches and put in the time to repeat and develop mastery, explore creatively. Push the limits, test your boundaries, and don't be afraid to be around people that can push you to the edge of what you are capable of becoming.

CHAPTER 5

Seven Rules for Dominating the Business Battlefield

Y OU CAN KNOW the rules to win in business, but here I want to provide you with the rules to absolutely dominate. To dominate something means that you have a commanding influence over it. When you are the best, people will come to you instead of you chasing after them. You are valued and respected because you have achieved what most will never. Success is rare. It takes us choosing what is unnatural so we can rise to a higher level. It takes us seeing what most can't see, and most importantly, it takes us having the courage to act off what we know to be true even though everyone and everything else around us is telling us otherwise.

STOP CARING ABOUT WHAT EVERYONE THINKS

You will never feel free until you can unchain from the grips that people have on your mind. This was one of the hardest things for me to learn. I was raised wanting to make my parents proud. Had my life not been flipped completely upside down when I was nineteen, I know I would not be where I am today.

My family completely cut me off. My mother had ten brothers and sisters on her side, and my father had eight siblings on his side. I grew up with family all around me, all the time. When my father cut his ties with me, the family chose him over me. I had a few aunts and uncles who kept in touch with me, but my family life has never been the same. It's always going to be different because I'm different now. I no longer fit in that cage anymore.

This was a major adjustment for me. I had to be OK being alone. A year after moving to the States, I got married, and I didn't want anyone to walk me down the aisle. I wanted to walk down with my Heavenly Father. This feeling of being alone was getting very familiar to me. It forced me to level up. I started to see the beauty in solitude. And at the same time, I knew I really was never alone. It started to become more and more evident to me that it's not about having as many people as possible around you, but instead it's about having the right people with you. The people who will never leave you.

When I was starting to learn about the insurance industry, imagine if I was still speaking to my family and actually cared what they thought. They would never be OK with me leaving my studies to become a doctor to instead get into business and become an entrepreneur.

This never goes away, even in business. I learned to stop asking for permission and just do what I knew was right. Why are you even asking someone for permission? If they actually knew what to do, they would be doing it.

My team is constantly innovating and doing different things. I never talk about what we do with anyone. First, because it's none of their business, but the real reason is everything outsiders say is just their opinion from their point of view of NOT DOING what I am doing. How could they possibly help me? They can't.

The majority of people on social media today are ill-equipped to be giving you advice in the first place. They haven't achieved much; they like the idea of being an influencer, but look at their lives—all you see is what they want you to see. Social media is just like media on television—it's not real life.

In my business, the team that I have is real. We are with one another. We work together as a unit to make the impossible happen every single week.

You need to make sure you are concerned with what the people who can actually help you think—and not everyone else.

If they can't help you pay your bills, you have no business listening to them.

STOP WORRYING ABOUT YOUR FAMILY

Understanding this is integral to eliminating weakness and taking control of your life. Never let your mom, dad, brothers, sisters, aunts, uncles, or cousins give you any advice if they are not equipped to do so.

Your spouse and your children must be one with you. You must get them aligned with your vision so they want to support you. On your climb up, don't expect support from anyone else in your family. It would be nice if those closest to you supported everything you do, but that's just not the way it goes. You need to know better. If you have a girlfriend or a boyfriend and they are already putting doubt in your mind, think long and hard about making that relationship permanent.

If you want to advance and you still live with your mom and dad, you won't go anywhere if they are on your back or unsupportive. People who grew up in a different era than you probably won't understand what is demanded of you to succeed today. You have to care more about your success than about how your family looks at you.

I say this because I was once heavily affected by the opinions of my family, and it wasn't until I learned how to turn that switch off that I was able to do great things.

Too many times I see people getting inappropriately involved in a person's business. They don't offer their support, and they make the work so difficult for people. If you are a spouse of someone who is in business, you need to be a part of that business in terms of support. There is so much that they have to learn and grow through. They don't need to be reminded of how hard it is—they already know.

On spouses...

As I said before, who you marry could be one of the MOST important decisions you make in your life. This has to be a union of two joined as one. That means one vision for the family. Make sure your values are aligned. Make sure there is a deep reverence for one another.

How do you deal with competing agendas? Don't have any. Your family cannot be competing for your time. They have to be supportive of what you are looking to accomplish. This will happen when you include your spouse and communicate this vision to them. I've seen it come in the form of women getting jealous that their husbands are working long hours and not spending time with them. I have also seen the reverse, where men are not supportive of women as they go and learn what it takes to become successful in business.

Spouses have to see work as a part of something that they are building for the family together, rather than competing for time or glory. In the beginning, the demands are high, and it takes the support of a spouse to understand that there is a promise they will achieve—but it comes with a price.

On children...

You are training your children in your actions and how they see you view work. Is there a positive energy associated with it, or do you have a negative outlook with it? Do you complain about leaving them and going to work, or do you show them you are excited to go to work? Do you explain to them that you are building something and working on achieving an accomplishment?

I grew up seeing my parents work so hard, and it automatically made me work really hard. I want my children to have that same instinct of great work ethic. I also want them to know that I enjoy what I do and work is a blessing to me.

On others...

Your family is your unit, meaning your spouse and your children. You have a duty and an obligation to get your spouse on the same page as you and make sure your children are led by you and you are not led by them. Everyone else is irrelevant. Cut them off. Put a pause on that relationship. Do what you must. Separation in this unit starts to happen when agendas start to drift apart and the vision of the family is misaligned. Instead of operating as one and with unity, division enters. Do everything in your power to guard and protect your family. A divided family can be the worst form of destruction. I believe that a family unit based on *perfect* love can withstand the difficulties of life because they understand that there is a greater vision together. It may be one of the greatest challenges of life to keep the bigger picture and unity rather than serving selfish agendas. We protect and defend what we love. The love of your family could be one of the most powerful driving forces you have. Take care of it.

STOP BEING OFFENDED AND START OFFENDING

While you are protesting, screaming in a microphone, and marching, someone else is working in overdrive to OWN YOU. That will be the ultimate offense.

Success is the ultimate platform to speak on. Work like no one else to achieve something great. Make your story be about how you won. No one wants to help someone complaining. More people care about helping people who are actively helping themselves.

Stop being a statistic. It's extremes that move things. You have to be rare and extreme in your pursuit of greatness to make a strong enough mark so that people will then want to actually listen to you. Otherwise, you become the noise of society, and eventually people start to tune this out—tune you out. Get people to tune into you. It's not about getting louder in your voice as much as it is about getting louder in your actions and results. People will respect you because of what you endured.

When we are protesting and marching, we are being a spectator to someone else's problems and issues. We do this because it gets us away from dealing with our OWN issues. It's easier to shine the light on someone else's problems rather than to shine a light on ourselves and what we have to do to improve. We are not participating in our own rescue.

"I used to have horrible cars that would always end up broken down on the highway. When I tried to flag someone down, nobody stopped. But if I pushed my own car, other drivers would get out and push with me. If you want help, help yourself—people like to see that."

—*Chris Rock*

POP YOUR BUBBLE

Ignorance is not always bliss. There are times where you need to have steely eyes and a fierce determination, where you are not distracted by the noise of the world. But you also have to be aware. You must cultivate great situational awareness.

In order to Stand Alone and lead your life, you need to have an understanding of what is really happening. Who is on your team? Who is rooting for you? And who is rooting against you? What is real and what is unreal? You must be able to dig deeper than most, instead of just existing on the surface. You need to be the one that goes through all the layers of what you are attempting to understand.

See the bigger picture. Most people only see what they want to see. Learn to Stand Alone and see what's actually there. When two people are communicating they are bringing in two different ideas, views, and perceptions of the situation. You must learn to leave your point of view and see from their point of view to be able to rise above the noise of people just defending their position or their point of view.

REALLY KNOW THY ENEMY

Everyone is not your friend. The closest people to you can turn on you and become your biggest enemies. Be careful who you let get really close to you. You have to be open to trusting people, but you have to be aware of the wolves dressed in sheep's clothing. People who pretend to be your friends and fans are more dangerous than your enemy because you at least know your declared enemy is your enemy. Be careful about the one who is pretending to be your friend and really conspiring against you.

Matthew 7:15–18

> *"Watch out for false prophets. They come to you in sheep's clothing, but inwardly they are ferocious wolves. By their fruit you will recognize them. Do people pick grapes from thornbushes, or figs from thistles? Likewise, every good tree bears good fruit, but a bad tree bears bad fruit. A good tree cannot bear bad fruit, and a bad tree cannot bear good fruit."*

The most powerful thing that you can control is yourself. Make sure that you are not doing wrong to others. Make sure to create an environment that does not permit people to get away with wrongdoing. Make sure that you are not looking at everyone else sideways and pointing out all their faults when you have more faults than them. No one likes a hypocrite.

The journey to becoming a better person will always start with us first. We must look within before we look on the outside for the source of where problems lie. This allows you to command respect, as opposed to demanding it.

People have to demand respect when they don't get any. Stop worrying about the respect that you don't get from people. When you work harder on yourself than anything else, you will have the ability to command respect from your environment and those who you wish to have around you. The right people will respect you, and the wrong ones never will.

There absolutely are people in this world who have an innocent and gentle persona on the outside and inside they are not about your best interests. Be especially careful with people that are charming. Flattery is the tool of the devil. They can lure you in with their charm, and it becomes really hard to see that they are capable of so much damage because they are so likeable. As you get more successful, this is something that you have to look out for. Unfortunately, this could happen with people you allowed to be very close to you.

So how do you know if someone is the real deal? Judge them by their fruits. As a society, we tend to be superficial, looking at the surface of things. When you Stand Alone, you have the ability to go a little deeper than most. Look to the inside of a person. What seeds have been planted in them, and what seeds do they wish to plant in your life? Does growing them grow more problems?

An apple seed can only produce other apples. When you squeeze an apple, apple juice comes out. This is why when life squeezes you, exactly what's inside of you is what will come out. Be aware of what people reproduce around you. Look at what they reproduce and believe what you see, not what you want to believe. Do the people around you sow seeds of prosperity or destruction?

SEEK THE TRUTH

To Stand Alone, you need to have thick skin in order to receive and give the truth. We all like the idea of the truth, but for many, the truth is too painful. That's why so many people have to anesthetize their existence so they don't have to ever really look at themselves or others in the face and deal with reality.

In order to be successful in business, you need to have the right people on your team. From years of interviewing tens of thousands of people, you start to see trends and patterns in people.

Often it takes time to see a person's true colors. In business, it will cost you a lot of money if you don't get to the truth fast. Money lost in training, bad deals, and bad decision-making. It all comes down to trust. Can you really trust the people on your team? Trust isn't built overnight, and it takes us giving trust to be able to ask for it. The best way to build this up is to endure challenging times with your people.

If you aren't building something important or doing much of anything, you don't need high levels of trust. You can just skip this part. But if you are looking to make a long and lasting impact, you need to have people around you who you can trust. Challenge your people and see if they will rise to the occasion. Do difficult things, and this is what will build bonds, a brotherhood and a sisterhood. With time, and while you are enduring these challenging tasks, the truth of the person will appear.

In BUD/S, the orientation to becoming a Navy SEAL—the toughest warriors on planet earth—candidates endure something called Hell Week. It's five and a half days of training with four hours total of sleep. This is being squeezed—on steroids.

"The entire training program is designed to eliminate quitters and those without the mental fortitude to push through when everything goes to hell," said Jason Redman Navy SEAL, Retired Navy Lieutenant.

There is something that all of us deeply admire about people who can endure and tolerate enormous amounts of stress without breaking. This is the highest level of trust.

I have had the privilege of speaking to a few Navy SEALs in my life, and it's really an honor to be in the presence of such greatness of people that live by a higher code.

Integrity is built into their ethos:

> *"I serve with honor on and off the battlefield. The ability to control my emotions and my actions, regardless of circumstance, sets me apart from others. Uncompromising integrity is my standard. My character and honor are steadfast. My word is my bond."*[1]

How many people really live by this ethos today? *My word is my bond.* I have made deals with people and shaken their hands only for them to go back against their word. It is the most distasteful thing to deal with.

I used to wonder why people lie. Then I learned that that's what liars do. We must trust but also verify in the business world because it's not always a Navy SEAL you will be shaking hands with. It's often, in fact, quite the opposite—cowards and wolves in sheep's clothing.

KNOW YOURSELF

Know what your strengths and weaknesses are and find people who complement you, regardless of how well you get along with them. Sometimes, the most difficult people are the ones you need to take

---

[1] "SEAL Ethos," Naval Special Warfare Command, United States Department of Defense, Accessed April 5, 2022, https://www.nsw.navy.mil/NSW/SEAL-Ethos/.

your life to another level. Grow your awareness of yourself and your environment.

Be the most real with yourself. A lot of people will tell you to focus on your strengths and forget about your weaknesses. I'm here to let you know that the enemy will attack you where you are weak. If you are not real about where you are weak and develop these areas, you leave yourself very vulnerable to be preyed upon by the enemy.

This is also where there is great power in learning how to work with other people who are nothing like you. When you can develop bonds with people who have different skill sets, they can strengthen you in areas where you are weak.

Are you better at working with people than working with data? In today's world, you have to be better than everyone else to win. Don't ignore the areas in which you are weak. That will erode your confidence and make you feel too reliant on someone else.

You should have the ability to learn but then also have the courage to put people in a position to flourish at what they are uniquely strong in and get out of their way. You still want to check in with them and make sure everything that you expect is being inspected to your standards.

The best way to get really real with yourself is to spend time alone with yourself. In a world that is constantly dinging at you, turn all your notifications off. Shut your phone off, get away from technology, and spend some time thinking about what really matters to you. This is a world where everyone is throwing their opinions on you. Think about what you believe, why you believe that, and then work on that. Start to align yourself with people who share your beliefs and values and grow in your conviction.

But never shy away from hearing people with opposing views. This can help strengthen you. Ask yourself: Why do you think and believe what you believe?

When I studied the great world religions, it gave me a window into why people think and act the way they do. Study different cultures and see why people behave the way they do. In being an open-minded person, you get to know yourself better. The most ignorant and weak people are the ones who are the most closed-minded. They think they know, but they really have no idea. A narrow mind is a destructive mind.

CHAPTER 6

Never Give
Your Power Away

I F YOU WANT to be treated with respect, then you must act respectfully. It's that simple. Ladies, you don't have to bat your eyelashes to get your way and men who work on their titles and muscles more than their brains are also dangerous. Instead, work on becoming a master of your craft. This chapter talks about your demeanor and how it affects your levels of success. The most important part of leadership is leading yourself. Leadership is a responsibility to do the right thing.

I see so many people become leaders on our team because they think they will make more money or have more power or because they want the title. These are the people who want the right thing for the wrong reasons, and they fail. They aren't ready to do what it takes.

When you are a leader, you give up the right to a private life because your entire life needs to be publicly led by example for your team. You can't preach that people should do the responsible thing while you are having casual sexual encounters with people at work, doing drugs, drinking, gambling, gossiping, or all of the above. What you do matters. The leader's actions set the tone for what is acceptable for the people they lead. If you don't like this, then don't be a leader. If you think your private life is no one's business, then don't be a leader. If you think you can do whatever you want and no one can tell you what to do—don't be a leader!

Leading by example is the most effective way to lead. I have had many people fail in this business, but the most disappointing failures are the people who could have done well if they were in control of their personal lives. Their problems outside of work ruin their professional lives, flushing all their hard work—and the investments of others around them—down the drain.

This chapter also covers how people change when they find success. When you come into any career, it takes a tremendous amount of work, energy, and time to get your skills up to par. It is a craft that requires continuous work and a drive to constantly improve. As you gain more and more success, you begin to find your flow, and it's a wonderful feeling, almost like you can do no wrong, that you can get away with anything. This is dangerous. I want you to know how to recognize this trend and overcome what has caused so many to fail.

The one person you can never run away from is yourself. What is *your* demeanor? How do *you* carry yourself? What do *you* internally identify yourself with? How you lead yourself will determine what you tolerate from those around you.

Do not be weak. I hate weakness. I hate seeing it in others, and I hate seeing it in myself. Do not tolerate weakness from others. Do not tolerate weakness in your team, in your family, in the people you have around you. We live in a world that celebrates failure and vulnerability. Why? Did you ever think that they have to do this to get you to start losing? What do they do to a cow before they slaughter it? They fatten it up and blind it.

We become fat because of one thing: EXCESS. You take in more than you are putting out, so fat appears. The only thing that I want to be fat in my life is my bank accounts. Everything else has to be mean and lean. But even money has to move. You earn it, and you have to move it so it can grow! Stagnation is death! When you Stand Alone, you are making a decision to produce more than you consume. Instead of letting life happen to you and letting random information just fall into your life, decide to create what you want out of life by actively pursuing what you want. Make a decision today to live a well-designed life.

You have to start looking at what you tolerate in your life. Do you allow stories in your mind to grow and to catch root? Your mindset is set by you when you become an adult. Your mind is like a fertile field. It's been pre-planted with seeds (values, beliefs, thoughts, and actions of our parents and others who we grew up with and were watching). If we keep watering these seeds, they will continue to grow.

Your power is from becoming self-aware—becoming self-aware to the programming of your parents and your parents' parents and the patterns, rituals, and habits that get passed down from generation to generation.

Did you ever wonder why you speak the way you speak? Can you listen to your own voice and hear what you sound like? What is an accent? Who creates that? Our environment does. We learn through and in our environment. Our environment is constantly feeding into us and shaping our thoughts, language, and actions. Music does this, too.

When you really take the power back in your life, you understand that YOU get to control your environment. If something isn't serving you, you can move, you can change direction, you can stop the planting. But make no mistake—someone is always planting something into your mind. We are all being programmed. The most powerful question you have to ask yourself is are you aware of this and what are you willing to do to change?

My parents knew this instinctively. We first lived in a small town called Scarborough in Ontario, Canada. It was getting more violent, so my father decided to move away from this city into one of the suburban areas. Like every child, we didn't want to leave our friends. We were comfortable where we were. We had been there so long. But my parents knew that if they were going to SET our minds right, they had to make a decision not out of comfort but out of putting us in a place that exposed us to greater things.

You meet people who never leave their hometown. It's all they know. What does that do to the mind? It keeps it very small. I believe the mind has infinite capabilities. But the environment shapes it. The exterior environment helps to mold the internal environment which controls our lives. What we are exposed to matters. It isn't about being comfortable. It's about getting around people and environments that make us uncomfortable so we can increase the set point of our mind and change our "normal."

Standing Alone is really about leadership. In order to lead ourselves, we must assess what current government we rule ourselves by.

The definition of government is the exercise of control or authority over a group of people. Before you examine which outside people are looking to control you, look at how you control yourself. Do you have a good internal government? If COVID taught me anything, it's the fact that who we elect as our representatives does matter. They create laws that govern and regulate what we can and cannot do. Are we OK with this? While some government is OK to have order and structure, unchecked governments are very dangerous.

The same is true for you. Look at your body as a fully operating system. All your body functions are talking to one another, giving feedback. The brain is the central government that directs and creates an orderly and functioning unit. But the power of the body is that it can get better. It's dynamic, not static.

We have to see this for our lives. For our lives to improve, sometimes we need to remind the government who is really in control. We have the ability to vote people in and out of office. The same is true for our mindset and our thoughts. We can vote thoughts in and out. Not everything we think has to pass as a bill, become the rule, and be enforced. The greatest countries in the world operate in a democracy where they can discuss what is better, listen to feedback, change, and improve.

Our lives are the same way. If all you did was listen to your brain, it would have you living in a corner almost like you are in jail. Your brain operates with an efficiency to keep you safe. If you did everything your brain wanted you to do, you wouldn't accomplish very much. The people who accomplish great things in this world override that safety mechanism in their brain and operate out of spirit.

So we must be able to govern ourselves. For people who are unable to govern themselves, it's very easy for a government to come and manipulate you. I want you to start manipulating yourself. Get in total control of yourself so that you NEVER EVER are controlled by other people and things.

What are the things that control most people? Money. Power. Sex. This is real. In the business world, if your personal affairs are not in order, then you run the risk of allowing other people to subject you to their weaknesses. Know what you value. Your values will rule over you like a government. They will determine what you tolerate, and what you tolerate will reproduce and grow. I made a decision that money, power, and sex will never overrule me. I value how God sees me far more.

As a woman in business coming up, I attended my first leadership summit. There was a male leader in a position of authority who told me there was more than one way to move up in this company. I was with another female at that time. This was after we were indoctrinated by this same individual telling us how to become a leader and how to lead other people. The decisions we make in a moment can affect us for a lifetime. Be careful of people that prey on your desire to achieve. People void of standards will test you. Make sure you pass. You must be governed by principles and not temporary feelings.

Nothing lasts forever except your soul. Make decisions from your soul.

The reality is, if I sold out on my soul, if I wasn't a person of faith, if I didn't have self-respect, if I didn't value honor and respect, I could have made some very bad decisions, if all I was chasing was a title. Instead, I look at this person today and OWN HIM. I know what he said. It's not the worst I have heard from men in business, but it was the first time when I went on a company trip and heard this. It made me really understand what really happens on some of those off-site company trips.

The price that I paid to keep my climb to the top free of any of this nonsense is PRICELESS. That's why I know no one has any control over me. I am controlled by something far greater. You must be controlled by something greater if you are looking to achieve something great.

It's getting harder for men to manipulate women. But I challenge all the women to toughen up and know who you are and never give in to those moments. They will come. It's just a matter of time. What will you do when it happens?

I've also met some women along the way who manipulate situations to their advantage. They work with men closely and then start to grow personal feelings for these men because they are in a position of authority. These women damage marriages as a result of not controlling their feelings and emotions. It may take two to tango, but it takes one to initiate, and one person has to have the courage to do what's right. Let that person be you. Always make decisions in business that you know in the long run you will be proud of.

When I think of my daughter, what do I want her to know? How will I teach her? When we have daughters and we put them in beauty pageants, what are we subconsciously teaching them? That you win based on the outside. That the game you are playing is one based on looks. And you wonder why women are so judgmental with one another. We literally teach them that they will be judged on their looks. That is an inevitable truth. As a human species, we will be judged from the outside. But we will win based on what's inside. That's why we have to work so hard on the inside.

I'm grateful my father never put me in beauty pageants. I love makeup. I love fashion. But I was learning how to pitch and catch, how to mow the lawn, and how to wash cars instead. I was introduced to books. My parents had a small shelf of chemistry books that I would stare at and get excited to read. I found joy in memorizing the periodic table of elements before I ever took a chemistry class. Do you know what that put into my subconscious? That everything is ordered and falls into a structure and a category based on its trends.

The universe is an orderly universe. Nothing happens without something first happening. For every cause, there is an effect. Every decision we make chisels out our character. Every time we make a bad decision, it follows us. It doesn't have to define us, but it does become a part of us. Nothing just happens.

At the end of life, where will you be placed? What category will you be lumped in? The one who gave this thing called life their all or the one dying with pounds of regret crushing their chest?

What trends will you follow? Will you be someone who walks through life with great order and structure, making decisions based on missions, values, and beliefs? Or will you do what is fast, easy, and trendy at the time to blend in with the masses or to get ahead faster instead of getting ahead by your own merit?

I hope you choose to stand up for your missions, principles, and values. I hope you choose to Stand Alone.

I've seen people who seem like they have everything going for them, and when I compared myself to them—if I were someone who had no principles or was void of good character—I would think it's only logical that I have to do something to manipulate an advantage for myself to catch up.

No.

Nature is the best balancing act ever played. Nature is not something to be played with or manipulated. Call it karma, destiny, or fate—it will boomerang back to you. For every action, there is an equal and opposite reaction.

I came to this country with a bag of clothes and a car. I didn't even have a home or a bed to sleep in. There was no government program that was going to help me. I had zero family members helping me pay my bills.

That's why no one owns me. The government doesn't own me. Men in power positions don't own me. No one in my family owns me.

I've been contracted under the same company for almost two decades. There are people who have done their best to make it incredibly difficult for me to advance. Being in business for almost two decades means that things have not always gone my way. When I think about what I'm building for the future, I go into it knowing that things will not always go as planned. But it will all work out in the end.

When I decided to start my own agency, everyone else was given three states to choose from. The day the call was happening to hear what states I would get to choose from so that I could take my money and open an office to sell products for an insurance company, they called and congratulated me and told me I was going to New York.

No one wanted to be in New York. It was expensive, and it was an animal all on its own. I had no idea all the problems that were associated with this territory, but I was about to find out.

When I asked what other states I would be given to choose from so I could take some time to think about it and go over this with my husband, I was told there weren't going to be any other options for me and there wasn't going to be anything to talk about.

I was told, "Either go to New York or you can stay where you are."

I ended up going to New York and renting an office in a great area in Long Island that I knew would do well. I was familiar with the area and knew what would be good for selling and the markets that I wanted to tap into to recruit to grow my business. After I put up a lot of my own money as a deposit for the new office, I found a home to move into and was excited to start this next chapter.

Then I got a phone call from my manager one evening telling me he was called and asked if he still wanted to keep me because I wasn't allowed to put an office where I selected and paid a nonrefundable deposit. I had to put my office where they wanted an office—in the Bronx, NY.

I had already put another deposit into a home that I would be renting. My career was being threatened by someone higher up. That night, I went looking for another job. It was the first time I did that.

I remember thinking, *What in the world is happening right now? Why is this happening?*

Who the hell are they talking to? The last time I checked, I was an independent contractor spending my own money to decide where I wanted to put an office to sell their company products.

The only thing that I never doubted was my abilities. I knew New York was a territory in which no one was succeeding, but I also knew that when people said something was impossible, I would find a way to get it done. This is where I do my best. I ended up making a deal to go into Westchester, New York instead of the Bronx. I lost all my deposit money in the other office in Long Island.

Westchester was a complete disaster. We would call people to recruit, and no one would come to our office. As soon as we gave them the address, they would hang up the phone on us, tell us that it wasn't really New York City, or just no-show the interview altogether. I knew I had to get out of there and fast. Every day that you waste in the beginning of your business as an entrepreneur is like a ton of bricks falling on your head. The longer you take to make progress and gain traction, the harder it will be to move. You have to put enormous amounts of energy into your work in the beginning to gain traction and results.

I finally got the courage to call the executive who sent me there and tell him this wasn't going to work and that I needed to move quickly. In business, when you are failing, fail fast. Don't drag it out. For all the mistakes I have made, I recognized them right away and corrected them with SPEED. This has saved me enormously. Too many people in business nurse their errors. This depletes your bank account and is a major reason why people file for bankruptcy or shut down altogether.

The day I told him I needed to get out of Westchester, you won't believe what he said to me: "I was waiting to see how long it was going to take you to realize that." Lesson—listen to that inner voice inside of you no matter how scary it may be.

The company had a closet-size office near Penn Station that they allowed me to use until I could find something better. They said I could use it because no one wanted to go into Manhattan, and no one had ever recruited from Manhattan and been successful because there are far too many issues with getting in and out of the city.

Perfect. Tell me no one can do something, and I will be that one.

We rocked it. We were outproducing everyone in NYC. We were crushing all of them in production.

And whenever you are winning, get ready for all the losers to come out of the woodwork to diminish your results. We started getting a lot of incident reports filed against us. An incident report is something that the public relations team files when a customer has a complaint. That means that they were saying my agents were generating complaints in the field with potential customers.

I would call these customers to follow up with them to see what the agent did wrong and hear more from the client, and the customers would tell me they never said that or that the incident never happened. When I brought this up to our home office, they responded by creating a rule that once an incident report is filed, we are no longer allowed to make any contact with that lead that we paid for. Isn't that convenient....

So I got labeled as someone who had too many PR complaints. When you get enough complaints, they start to give you fewer leads to work with. We were getting fewer and fewer—until we were getting almost zero. I had a large team with no resources to give to them. I had to learn to become resourceful. What do you when there is no one to help you? What do you do when it feels like everyone is working against you? It felt as though I was being squeezed out of the territory, going from producing the most to producing the least. What do you do? Stand Alone and see it as a blessing.

That's because it is. That's how a lot of businesses operate. There's a lot of politics, a lot of inside-operations shenanigans, and if you are not aware, you will start to go crazy. It's the things you don't know that will absolutely hurt you.

Look at our own government today. What a disgrace. Businesses are no different. People in power who shouldn't be in power manipulated their way to get there, so they continue to manipulate their way to STAY in power. But who ends up winning? You, if you can just keep doing the right thing.

In that moment, I had to make a decision to learn a new way of doing business. A way that I could keep myself sustainable and not ever be dependent on anyone else ever again. I started calling major organizations and started prospecting with businesses, sponsoring large events, and getting very creative to be able to generate my own leads.

The greatest resource on planet earth is resourcefulness. Learning how to take care of yourself. Knowing that no one is coming to rescue you. Being the kind of person who makes a decision to find a way to make it happen.

I failed.

I failed miserably. I was so overwhelmed. The money that I had to find to pay personal expenses and keep the business open all came crashing down on me. Every month, I would have to tap into our emergency life savings to keep the business open for one more month. It was so bad at one time I remember finding cash in the house and going to the bank and depositing it to help pay the bills. I was drowning and fast.

Paying for a home and office in New York City was no joke. I didn't have time on my side. My expenses for one month in New York were maybe six months' worth of expenses somewhere else. I reached out to the company and asked for help. Crickets.

The one thing I never doubted in myself was my ability to produce results. I felt as though there were too many things working against me and that I needed to make a move.

When the company heard I was leaving the territory, they did everything to get me to stay. I wouldn't do it because I gave my word to someone else that I was leaving.

I eventually ended up in Chicago, Illinois. The president at that time, Scott Smith, saved my life. He gave me a chance to redeem myself when no one else wanted to. I don't know why help comes at some times in our life and then at others it feels like we are being hung to dry. All I know is that when you keep moving, you will get to a place in your life when you can look back and see those moments of God's grace in your life.

God's grace—receiving something you don't deserve.

When I arrived in Chicago, I made a vow to myself and God that NOTHING for the next ten years was going to move me from here. I would stay, I would persist, and I would win. I went on a ten-year campaign to never be dependent on anyone for anything. Over ten years later, it was the best decision I ever made. It was the most gratifying ten years of my career!

Everything that I had been through prior to coming to Chicago helped to serve me. It helped me to look at everything from a different point of view. The hardships of those prior years helped to build the resolve that was needed to win.

This is real life. This is what happens in business. This is the stuff that no one talks about because we'd rather share Instagrammable moments that make us look perfect. These are the reasons why many people don't make it in business.

Business is ruthless. It always has been. You need to have a stomach for this. No matter what you are going through, have principles and values that you hold on to. Let those guide you, not people. People will fail you. People who you think you can trust can turn on you. People lie. They say terrible things. Never give any of your power to them. What they call you is what they are. Don't let it affect you. Let it serve you. Use it as fuel to help you propel yourself forward.

I own all the space in my head. I'm so glad I never gave any of my power away. I'm so glad I kept on going when they tried to make me think I'm crazy. I'm glad I already knew who I was.

Stand Alone and know who you are. Never give your power away to anyone.

CHAPTER 7

Move from Products to People

Proverbs 27

Wounds from a friend can be trusted,
but an enemy multiplies kisses.

Be sure you know the condition of your flocks,
give careful attention to your herds;

for riches do not endure forever,
and a crown is not secure for all generations.

YOU CANNOT AMASS a fortune through business until you move from working with things to working with and developing people. In this chapter, I cover the essential skills of working with people. My career would not be the same if I'd never implemented this in my own life. When I started in sales, I had one task at hand: to become good at sales. At its essence, being in sales is about generating revenue for your company. Salespeople are vital to every organization. Without them, even a company that makes the best product is dead in the water.

I worked my butt off, read every book, and became the most successful salesperson in my company. I thought I knew everything I needed to know when I got my promotion, but all of that changed when I got into leadership. I made a decent income in sales, but leadership is where I began earning a fortune.

Most people feel bad talking about money and people in the same sentence. You can't. They are intrinsically connected. Money is nothing without people. We move it. We choose what we do with it. We give it value. It is nothing without us. In business—not at your home, not in the eyes of your family, not in the eyes of God—you are nothing without money. Money breathes life into people. It provides a source of energy, fuels a level of creativity, and gets you to open up to different environments, people, and networks. People and money go hand in hand. The people who are the most successful in business are not just good at selling products, they are also amazing at working, dealing with, and leading people. It's not easy, and that's why the pay is so high—because the skill is so valuable. This skill is also very rare.

It wasn't until I started studying people—what makes them tick, what moves them, what inspires them, and what motivates them to do what they do—that my career really took off. Learning to work with people and caring about developing and growing them is one of the most important skills to have if you expect to do exceptional things in this lifetime. When you learn how to work with people, you can adapt to different environments. You're given access to someone with more than just great ideas they can't communicate or execute through others. It's an absolutely essential skill that revolutionized my life.

The hardest thing to do in business (or on a sports team) is to develop people. It's easier to just snatch up talent. The only problem with that is that they have no loyalty to you. Empires are built when people are there for more than just a short-term advancement. Look at the Bulls and the dynasty that was created. The owner, the coach, the players, and the stars on the team understood the dynamics, and they played together to win. When aligned, the magic happens. Then usually what happens is corporate comes in and looks at people as interchangeable parts. They look at people that way because they have never really developed and stuck with someone through good and bad. They didn't take someone from a baby in the business to a titan, so they don't understand what ownership really means.

For the most part, these are salary people who are put into a corporation for a period of time and have an agenda. Their agenda is their stock prices. They look at everything like inputs and outputs. People are data points to them. They have no idea what culture is about. You talk to them about building people, which takes time, and they look at you like you are an alien speaking a different language—because you are. Corporate people and players in the game are different people. They are not made of the same material. When a player starts playing like a corporate piece versus actually being a team player, you get someone like Lebron James who can hop around from team to team, chasing the win at the expense of their team.

The people who are building an empire go through a lot together. They are bonded differently. They have different agreements with one another. Imagine how much a team the Bulls were for Michael Jordan—the greatest of all time—to say, "I'm not playing if he's not my coach." Players today can't and won't understand this mentality. That's why the Bulls won as much as they won—because they knew they weren't playing forever. It was about the team playing together as one. This is rare. This is not how the majority of teams operate.

But this is how championship teams operate. They are all or nothing. They completely have each other's backs. This is THE hardest thing to create in a culture. The team takes a priority over any one individual. People who are good with numbers do not create these environments. People who are good with PEOPLE create this. When you are good at both, you are RARE!

In the insurance industry, the hardest part is what it takes to grow and develop the people on your team. After you sell someone on the idea of selling life insurance, you then have to get them to go and take their exam and get properly licensed to work a 100 percent commission job. And it's a job that will make you work as you have never worked in your life before. Why do you think the entire personal development industry was created by people in the life insurance industry? It's true. Imagine selling a product that people can't touch, that they will never get to see the benefit of until they are dead? We have to be pretty damn good to do what we do. There isn't a better place to put your money to protect your family from a tragedy or to protect your wealth and keep it tax-free at death, but it isn't an easy sell.

That's why people who work in this industry would rather steal people and promise them higher commissions rather than grow, develop, and keep people over time. I have come to learn that there is money everywhere. Why you do what you do has to matter more than the money. The next thing that has to matter is WHO you are doing it with. If you are winning on a team that really isn't a team, why does it matter? If people want more money today, they don't work harder at their skills to become more valuable to the organization. Instead, they are being told to ask their boss for more money. If you don't get it, leave and go somewhere else. The problem with this strategy is that you will end up unhappy again, and then what are you going to do? Leave again?

Great teams possess a high-performance culture. They have such high standards that they don't lower their standards to meet anyone's expectations. They keep their standards high and demand that you rise up to their standards or you won't be a good fit for that team. Great teams also have great coaches that reinforce this. They are not afraid to tell everyone on the team what they need to hear. The teams that lose are more focused on the feelings of the players rather than their outcomes.

Do you want someone to charm you or to chisel you? Are people telling you what you want to hear? Filling you with fluff and making you a cream puff? Making you feel better than you actually are? What they are really doing is fattening you up for the slaughter. The greatest coaches will make you lean and mean. They will make sure that you are developed as a person both inside and out. They will work on your character and spiritual growth just as much as your physical growth. They will increase your capacity to handle more and ultimately get you to perform at the edge of your capabilities. They will get you to do what you would never do on your own.

How many people would choose to hear words that cut you from someone who really cares about your growth and development? Not many. That's why most people today prefer to hear the words of someone who is soothing and can relate to them. Your misery likes company, and when you are down on yourself, you search for this. Great cultures, great teams, great players, and great coaches won't provide this for you. They will provide an environment that gets you to make a shift in your thinking. Instead of relating to you, they will challenge you, which can then change you. So if you are in pursuit of your greatest self, seek out someone stronger—a coach, a team, and other players—who won't be afraid to push you, challenge you, and develop you.

Those environments that are the most comfortable are silently killing our spirits. It feels good for a while, until you realize that you could have done more, you could have become something more. If you are a leader, you must constantly be challenging yourself. Your team is watching to see what you are doing to take your game to the next level. After you win, how will you follow it up with another win? This inspires them to do the same. This creates a culture of people who are willing to push themselves to do and become better. If you are a parent, your children are inspired by watching you achieve great things. This sets the tone and example for them to follow. No child is inspired by their parents watching TV; they want to know what their parents are doing right now.

Your dedication and hard work don't go unnoticed by them; it feeds into them, and it will create a culture within your family that will hopefully serve you for generations to come. Tough environments and people who have the courage to speak the truth are what we need more of. Whatever you have been through, let it serve you. It was brought into your life not to break you but to make you come out stronger and to be an example for others to follow.

CHAPTER 8

Evolve or DIE

N o business cares what you did in the past if it's irrelevant today. More than anything, a business wants to know if you are capable of learning. The days of hiding behind the cubicle walls are over. It's easy to recognize people who are stuck. They literally cycle through life with the same things happening to them over and over again because they never learn or change.

When I see people in business who are like this, it infuriates me. This type of person costs your business much more than you can calculate. Their curse on your business is insidious. They are taking their sweet time to learn on your dime, and if you don't call them out on it, they will never change, and it will run your business into the ground.

This chapter shows you how to recognize these people and either help them change or replace them. They are a liability to your organization, and I will also show you how to get rid of them before they take everything you taught them (along with their contact list) to a competitor.

Change is not easy, but you need to see your people make an effort to adapt to the new way of business, or it will cost you your culture. That is something you never want to leave in the hands of someone else. Being a leader means that you have to set a vision and create a culture that supports that vision coming to life.

This chapter also discusses loyalty and creating a culture that encourages it. You must learn to study people and anticipate their actions before they even engage in them. One of the easiest ways to test your team's loyalty is to implement change and see if they will work through it with you or bounce.

When you are in a sales environment, you really understand that you have to produce daily. I think everyone should look at their job like a commission. People today associate a negative feeling with getting paid a commission. Maybe that's because you want some sort of guarantee or room to wiggle. When you are on commission, there is no room to wiggle. If you don't work, you don't get paid.

com·mis·sion
/kə'miSHən/

1. *an instruction, command, or duty given to a person or group of people. "He received a commission to act as an informer"*

2. *a group of people officially charged with a particular function.*

Michelangelo was commissioned by the Vatican to produce one of the greatest works of art: the Sistine Chapel. Being paid a commission is about performing. It's not the same as someone who is just doing their job. A commission is a calling. When you interview for a calling, you aren't interested in how many sick days and paid vacation you get. A calling is something you feel a charge to do.

This is why people get into business and become entrepreneurs. There is something calling them to take more risks. To leave the safety net of a "job" with benefits to carve out their own lane in a world that produces so many failed businesses. Stats show that 20 percent of new businesses fail within their first two years, and only 25 percent of new businesses make it to fifteen years or more.[2]

The longer you stay in business, the more likely you are to not make it. Every new year will bring new challenges that can take you under. If you fail to innovate and stay ahead of these changes, you will always be reacting and behind. When you fall too far behind, it gets harder and harder to see your way out. You have to stay ahead. Movement in business is life. Stagnation and stasis are death. That's why it takes a warrior spirit to win in business. We have to be operating from a higher sense of purpose if we are about to do something that seems impossible. Comfort is our enemy.

When you are in business and you think you have made it, you are called to find a better way. The people who stay in business are the ones who are constantly pushing the limit and working on becoming better, never accepting the status quo. We learn to hunt and fish for our own food. The easier path doesn't activate the warrior spirit that it takes to win in business. That's why you need to constantly be innovating.

What does it mean to innovate? It means to disrupt. Disrupt yourself. Disrupt the current way you do business.

On my team, we are constantly learning and sharpening our skills. We never get complacent, and we train every day to get better and

2   Michael T. Deane, "Top 6 Reasons New Businesses Fail," Investopedia, January 10, 2022, https://www.investopedia.com/financial-edge/1010/top-6-reasons-new-businesses-fail.aspx#:~:text=Data%20from%20the%20BLS%20shows,to%2015%20years%20or%20more.

better. That's why if you meet one of my agents versus another agent in the industry, there is no question that we will smoke you. The ability to hunt and train is key to lasting and thriving in business. We are a high-functioning team that constantly needs to be sharpened. None of us feels like we have arrived. We are always training for the next best thing. That means that everyone copies us. That's OK. When you figure out what we are doing, you will be where we were. We are constantly moving. Movement is life. Success is fragile, and it can get stale if you stop moving.

If you've ever stayed in a city before, it's inspiring. A city is a high concentration of people who are overachieving. How do the beautiful skylines of world class cities form? One building at a time. But it takes the best wanting to build their best to create a building that will stand out, be iconic, and win awards. And after one goes up, someone builds another. They build the next building taller, more innovative, with the intention of getting noticed and changing—disrupting—that skyline. When the building is so great, it becomes a symbol of greatness. Every major city has this. New York has the Chrysler Building and the Empire State Building. Chicago has the Willis Tower. Dubai has the Burg Khalifa (which was inspired by the iconic Trump Towers in Chicago—but taken to a whole different level).

Evolving is about first being inspired. This is why to be successful we often model someone else who is successful in our same field and industry, but then we take it to the next level. We make it better. That's what innovators do. If you can't evolve, you run the risk of being the same as everyone else and dying out. Life isn't about blending in—it's about standing out. But you first have to have a solid foundation to stand on before you attempt to stand out. When I came into the insurance industry, I was given leads, people to go and see. These were referrals of old agents who had quit and left the company. They were a nightmare to call. We also had access to people who worked in a union who filled out a card to be seen and requested to be delivered a basic accidental program. These people were also a nightmare, not because they were bad people but because of how they were set up to be seen.

I learned very quickly that when you aren't transparent in sales, it doesn't help—it hurts. People who try to be tricky and manipulative in sales can never last. They do this because they are not good at selling what they sell. When you have to manipulate and trick people into buying what you are selling, it means that you are not good at what you are selling or you don't believe that the product you are selling is very good. Either way, in order to be successful in sales you have to fully believe in yourself, the product you sell, and the company that you represent.

The whole point of selling is to make people want what you have, then it has to make logical sense for them to keep it. When you are collecting referrals in business, it's about delivering such good service and presenting so well that the customer WANTS their family and friends to have the same products and experience that they just had. It becomes a privilege for them to gift someone else with what they just received. The customer is buying your conviction and referring their experience to others. To excel at sales, you have to work the hardest on sharpening your skills every single say. And you have to make sure that you are delivering an experience that goes above and beyond, so that the customer wants to give you referrals. Without referrals in any business, you won't be in business for long.

Peter Drucker said, "Because the purpose of business is to create a customer, the business enterprise has two—and only two—basic functions: marketing and innovation. Marketing and innovation produce results; all the rest are costs. Marketing is the distinguishing, unique function of the business." Marketing is all about the customer experience. How did you make them feel? A person who feels good about themselves makes good decisions. Most people think marketing has to do with tricks, but what it really has to do with is human behavior. Making sure you understand the customer, their wants and needs. As for the innovation part of business, this really starts with you. Do you care to be the best? Do you care to put in the enormous work to perfect your craft when no one is watching so that you can differentiate yourself from others who are ordinary and just doing what they have to?

The customer must become a raving fan of yours. Raving fans spread the word. Being successful in sales means that you accumulate multiple raving fans so that you have disciples spreading the word for you. Think about how Jesus spread His word. He didn't have access to a press release, let alone a printing press, to get his word out. Christianity spread without the radio, TV, or social media. He relied on a handful of people who believed in his mission. Now that people have social media in their possession, word travels a lot faster and a lot farther than it ever did before. That's why you have to be so much better than in the past. We are all exposed. We have to add TREMENDOUS value to our customers. If you do something unethical to try to trick or manipulate someone, you won't last. You will get exposed, and fast!

And that's a good thing. It creates a marketplace where people want real and authentic. We have a nose for fakes. We have no tolerance for people who are just copying someone else. We want to reward the originals. Consumers want to be a part of something. Something rare and unique that makes them feel special.

The disciples of Jesus were commissioned by Him to spread the good news. It worked. They were doing things differently at that time, and it caught on. Jesus gathered men from very different backgrounds and told them He wasn't just going to feed them but rather teach them how to fish for themselves. He also told them that He would make them fishers of men. They even had a symbol of a fish that was adopted by the earliest Christians—the ichthys. The ichthys was used especially when Christians were being persecuted by the Romans and wanted to know if someone they were meeting with was a fellow believer in Christianity.[3]

The Christians were commissioned to become "fishers of men." They were officially charged. How about you? Do you feel charged in your work? Are you constantly playing to win and make a difference, or do you find yourself struggling to keep up with the status quo? When you stop innovating and evolving, you run the risk of losing. We first lose our creativity, and then the loss of creativity will cost us our entire business. Winning requires an "ALL IN" mentality. People fail in sales jobs every day because they fail to be in commission. They try to work a sales job like an ordinary job. It won't work. People who run insurance companies are always trying to make it easier for people to get into sales. They lower the barrier of entry—so low that it becomes uninspiring to work in the industry.

The truth is, it takes you being an extraordinary person to make it in sales.

On our team, we only want to work with the extraordinary—people who are willing to be on a mission and a calling rather than just exist. We evolved from the regular ways of growing a sales organization and wanted to work with the best of the best. We wanted to teach people how to fish instead of feeding them and creating a welfare state in our office. We chose to set our standards high, and we let everyone who decides to join our team know that it's up to them to raise their standards to meet up with us—we will never lower our standards to meet with them. Be great or be gone!

---

[3]   Collin Hansen, "Story Behind," *Christian History Institute*, 2004, https://christianhistoryinstitute.org/magazine/article/story-behind.

The best leaders understand that they have to have empathy, but we have zero sympathy. Having empathy means we have an understanding of where a person is coming from. We need to have this understanding to help to guide people to a better place. Sympathy is something different. Great leaders don't feel sorry for anyone. We had our own struggles and we overcame them. We know that if we make everything easier, it will just produce weakness. What makes a great leader great is when you overcome something very challenging and you can relate to those that are currently in a difficult place, but you can also be that person who is inspiring to them by showing them that if you did it, so can they. The role of a leader is not to do anything for you, it's to guide you, to be an example for you. The best leaders overcome massive hardship—that's why we are inspired by their stories.

When I was in New York, we were winning, and then everything started to take a turn for the worse. We were heavily dependent on the lead system provided by the company. We were being blamed for all the groups having issues and being lost because of the number of complaints we were receiving. I wasn't allowed to call the customers, so it was just our word against theirs. This is never a good thing. The problem with the setup of the lead is that the process was not transparent.

Union members were being told to fill out a card for a small accident policy and our job as agents was to go and upgrade them with an individual life insurance policy. The PR team got paid for the amount of cards that came in, and the agent got paid if he or she could sell a life insurance policy to them.

Two groups were commissioned to do two totally different things.

You can see why there was a problem here. No alignment. The PR would tell the members that they just needed to fill out the card. We would go to homes, and the union members would tell us that they were told they didn't have to meet with us if they didn't want to. Imagine if the groups were set up to understand the products that were being made available to them and how they would benefit them versus just getting as many cards filled out as possible? The PR team would also team up with school districts in low-income areas, and we would catch them paying for pizza parties if the teacher would just fill out all the cards with the parent information on them. When the agents would call these homes, the families had no idea what was going on, and it would be a constant issue of building trust with the family from the beginning of the presentation.

Everything eventually came to a screeching halt. The unions no longer wanted to do business with our company, and I was slammed for this. So what did I do? I started to learn how to run my own events and not become dependent on the company for leads. I started to teach my agents how to do events and build their own supply of leads. The NY PR team would find our boxes that we would leave in schools and businesses, and it became another issue. We were no longer allowed to generate leads in the schools. So I decided to sponsor community events. We did an event, and one of the PR reps from corporate decided to come see what we were doing. We had agents collecting leads, and I gave her a clipboard and told her to get to it—help get some leads.

She came to me and said, "I don't know how you are doing this. I can't get anyone's name." During that one event, we collected 2000 leads. And she contributed zero. I knew I didn't need them anymore. But it never felt right. The territory was tainted because the leadership was incompetent. I asked to speak to the president and vice president at the time to express what I was feeling, and they didn't want to hear it. They were not interested in my problems. I decided I didn't want to be in this territory anymore. Why was I paying a premium to have an office in the most expensive place in the USA with their name on it with zero support? It's one thing to have no support, but it's a whole different feeling when you are being set up for something and held responsible for something that is not accurate. My team was being blamed for losing all these poorly set-up groups.

I sent an email to the vice president explaining that I no longer wished to be in this territory and that I was going to move on. I never questioned my capabilities. I started to question who I was working with. When you are on commission and you are highly skilled, you care about who you are working with. Do they care about you? Do they see you? Do they value you? They started to value me after I said I was leaving. I made a deal with someone that I would help to grow their team and we could partner and build something incredible together. I shook another man's hand and made a deal to relocate. After that, I was told that none of the PR issues were my fault. I was offered money to stay. A part of me wished I had never made a deal with someone else, but I stayed true to my word with this other person. I shook their hand and told them I was going to work with them, so I kept my promise.

I learned that you have to get everything documented. Put it in writing, and even then, people still lie. You can sit and get caught up in your feelings, or you can move on. I knew I had to move on. I spent the next decade building a business in Illinois. But I started with one thing in mind: to be a referral-based business. I was not going to be dependent on anyone to be in control of my business but me.

From day one, I hired and trained agents to work on referrals. We have mastered the art of events. We are constantly pushing the limits of what we can do and evolving our customer base. We have fallen in love with our customer and not our products—and our customers love us back. We have become the highest-producing team in the history of this territory. Because of our success, we weren't celebrated. The home office decided to put ten other competitors in our backyard to take a piece of our pie. Little did they know, we moved on to bigger and better things. Every single team that has come into this territory promised big things—talked a big game—but in the end, they couldn't make it. They couldn't last.

We did make it and we moved on, all because we never got stuck. We are continuously working on improving and innovating to become better. You can't disrupt a disruptor. All I can say is that the business world is ruthless. People smile in your face and stab you behind your back. That is the nature of business. Anyone who thinks business isn't a war will be the first to fall into submission and surrender. You have to have the stomach for it. You shouldn't take things personally, but the best make it all personal. Success truly is the best revenge, but it doesn't happen overnight. It's going to test everything you think you know and understand about people. The people who you think you should be able to trust the most WILL betray you. What you see and what people show you about themselves is only a fraction of who they really are. You will continue to get played if you don't look deeper than what people choose to reveal to you.

Remember in New York, how they started lying about my team and making up incident reports that I would call about and that customer said the incident never happened? Fast forward another ten years in Chicago, and they tried to pull my policyholders from me and give them to a competitor because they told another union president that my team was to blame for making their members upset. I brought this up to the company and the head of PR. I knew this was another lie, and they were using my team to throw us under the bus to advance themselves. It took many meetings to finally get to the truth.

What's the difference between New York and Chicago? I evolved as a business owner. I stopped playing from defense and made a decision to operate from a place of truth and courage, standing up for myself and my team. You either stand up for what is right or allow people to roll right over you. We are commissioned and called to do what has never been done before.

I am grateful that my team trusts me. I have never taken their trust lightly. I know what that feels like, and I refuse to do that to another. What good is a leader who has no trust with their team? I am honored to have a team that may not always agree with me, but, with time, they have come to see that everything falls into place and that the vision I have is further than most can see, and we trust one another to walk toward it together no matter how uncomfortable it can get at times. We have taken some massive hits as a team, and I am sure there are more to come. As long as we have trust, there is nothing we won't be able to overcome. Business is ruthless. Being in business with people you can't trust is impossible. The future of business will belong to those who can work with transparency, character, and competence.

CHAPTER 9

Betrayal: Don't Worry, EVERYONE is Replaceable

N EVER, EVER FORGET that you can be replaced immediately. There is someone younger, better educated, and willing to take a lower salary who is just waiting for your position. People do well and get complacent—and then they get replaced. Growth is a must. Work on becoming hard to be replaced but carry humility in your heart.

The danger with success is that we think it's all because of us. But a business will move on, with or without you. The principle of "nature abhors a vacuum" is very real, especially with businesses. When we earn enough success or money or clout, we start to think that nothing could function without us. This just isn't true. In a world that places so much value on each individual human, we can get this message confused and start to think we are more than we are. This is a very dangerous mindset to have. Entitlement is a drug that is more potent than any controlled substance on the market.

This chapter shows that when you have people on your team growing heads bigger than the entire organization, you must cut them loose—and on your terms. While swallowing even one cell infected with HIV would be unthinkable, managers everywhere resist pulling the plug on people who are walking infections within their culture. Not me. Just as HIV weakens your immune system, these people will compromise your entire organization. You need to get them out. This chapter talks about protecting your people and your business so that you don't suffer at the hands (and mouths) of those who want to do you harm.

Everyone has a Judas. Who was Judas to Jesus? He was a close disciple of His, but he wasn't one of the closest. Why is that? Did Jesus know something? Did He feel something about him? At His last Passover dinner, Jesus found the courage to confront his own disciples. He wanted them to know that He knew.

"And while they were eating, he said, 'Truly I tell you, one of you will betray me.'" (*Matthew 26:21*)

The response of Judas was, "Surely you don't mean me, Rabbi?" (*Matthew 26:25*)

There are some who will sell you for personal gain. That's expected. We live in a society that is very jealous. Whenever people spend more time consuming than creating, there is a void created that gets filled with jealousy.

It's the woman who looks at a married man, wishing that he was her husband. It's the man who demeans another man because he feels physically powerless against him, so he asserts his power in other cowardly ways. It's your friend who smiles on the outside but wishes you the worst possible things on the inside. Not everyone is like this, but you would be naïve to think that there aren't a few who are. The closer they are, the more it will hurt. Judas wasn't the only one who turned on Jesus. Many did. We know the deep remorse they felt because of how close they were to Him.

Peter was told by Jesus, "This very night you will all fall away on account for me, for it is written." (*Matthew 26:31*)

Peter denied the words of Jesus. Never say never.

"Peter replied, 'Even if all fall away on account of you, I never will.'" (*Matthew 26:33*)

Loyalty isn't a word. It's an action. What do you do when the person who is closest to you, the one you trust the most, betrays you? In this case, it happened three times.

Peter reinforced his stance in a declaration to Jesus, "Even if I have to die with you, I will never disown you." (*Matthew 26:35*)

I have had people so close to me betray me. Had I not known the story of Jesus, it probably would have broken me. The hardest thing I ever went through was the abandonment of my parents. Looking back, I fully realize that their void in my life allowed me to grow into a whole new person. Like a caterpillar in a cocoon undergoing a metamorphosis, I built a shell around myself. There was no one to help me. And that's why I came out winning.

If you assist the butterfly and help to cut the cocoon to aid in its release, the wings of the butterfly fail to develop because they lost the chance to develop by the pressure of pushing against the cocoon to strengthen its muscles. That time in my cocoon strengthened my muscles. Every single person who betrayed me ultimately didn't affect me because I endured it at the highest level with my parents.

What we learn from the story of Jesus has two different outcomes. The first outcome is what happened to Judas.

"When Judas, who had betrayed him, saw that Jesus was condemned, he was seized with remorse, and returned the thirty pieces of silver to the chief priests and the elders." (*Matthew 27:3*)

The elders refused to receive the money—it was blood money, and they didn't want to be associated with it. Judas ended up throwing the money into the temple and hanging himself.

What makes someone betray someone so close to them for a temporary advance? We don't know because we never get to hear the side of Judas. What we do know is that Jesus didn't worry about him. He knew that Judas would take care of himself.

So, too, with your enemies. Do what's right. They will get theirs. They always do.

Why did Jesus know what his friends would do and still let them do it anyways?

Judas arranged to give a sign to the chief priests and the elders of the people—a signal to point out Jesus to them so they could arrest Him.

"The one I kiss is the man; arrest him." (*Matthew 26:48*)

When Judas saw Jesus, he approached Him with greetings and kissed Him. Jesus replied to him and said, "Do what you came for, friend." (*Matthew 26:50*)

OUCH.

What does it mean to live on purpose and on a mission that is higher than what you are currently going through at the time? I am grateful that I have this story to always reflect on, because I can tell you I have gone through times in my life with such high levels of betrayal that made me realize what was happening was all a part of the plan.

Loyalty isn't tested in good times. It's tested and showcased in the worst of times. And in the words of Maya Angelou, "When someone shows you who they are, believe them."

How was Jesus able to stay in His mission knowing that He was about to endure such betrayal from those who were closest to Him? In watching how Jesus handled Himself, we come to understand that this is human nature. We also come to understand that the betrayer is always the one who suffers the most when all is said and done. The most important thing to understand about betrayal is that it's more about who the betrayer is and really has very little to do with you. When you are on a mission, these instances can serve as a great distraction. For me, they brought tremendous hurt and pain. But you must guard your heart and continue to press forward.

The Bible tells us to guard our hearts. (*Proverbs 4:23–27*)

> *Above all else, guard your heart,*
> *for everything you do flows from it.*
> *Keep your mouth free of perversity;*
> *keep corrupt talk far from your lips.*
> *Let your eyes look straight ahead;*
> *fix your gaze directly before you.*
> *Give careful thought to the paths for your feet*
> *and be steadfast in all your ways.*
> *Do not turn to the right or the left;*
> *keep your foot from evil.*

In business and in life, one thing is inevitable. It involves working and dealing with people. People are simple and complex all at the same time.

We can't build a wall around people to protect ourselves from ever getting hurt. The wall that we put up may very well keep all the bad out, but the same wall will also keep all the good out.

But you can learn to read people. Not everyone is your friend, and not everyone has your best interests at heart. The most dangerous people aren't the ones who let you know they are dangerous. In fact, those are the ones you can trust the most. What you can't trust and what you should become more aware of are the people who greet you with kisses but plot against you.

I had an assistant for many years, and she was someone into whom I placed a deep level of trust. I found out that she was stealing a lot of money from me. She admitted to stealing the money because she knew I was on to her. She couldn't sleep anymore. She came into my office one morning and asked to speak to me. She smelled of death. She said she would pay the money back. I told her she had to leave. She didn't pay the money back. She lied to the police and used COVID as an excuse to not face them. The police department in the town we were working in was completely incompetent, so I took her to court. The court system is comprised of another group of even more incompetent people of whom lawyers take complete advantage, taking cases and stretching them out as long as possible to keep billing and billing.

What does a lack of trust cost you? More than you will ever calculate. The feeling of betrayal, the energy, the time, the money—it's all so wasteful. Guard your heart—and also guard your inner circle—very well.

When you steal something from someone, you display to the world how weak you are. You also display how immature you are as well. Why is it that all kids steal? Because they want to see what they can get away with. If they have parents who fail to discipline them and therefore teach them that there are no consequences for their actions or their lack of respect for authority, society will ultimately have to pay. Then this kid lands in a business, and the business owner is caught teaching that "child" a lesson (or someone else will have to pay).

How many criminal charges and lawsuits drain unnecessary energy and attention from people looking to be productive and creative instead of putting energy into someone trying to destroy them?

Again, we can look to the human body to see that you need both systems in working order to be healthy. Our body has two systems: a sympathetic nervous system and a parasympathetic nervous system. Infections are real and so are bad people. You are in an optimal state when your body can go back and forth to encourage growth and also to protect you. Our autonomic nervous system uses both the sympathetic nervous system (SNS) and parasympathetic nervous system (PNS) to keep us alive.

In the simplest terms, think about the SNS as the system that prepares your body for fight or flight. When you are in a situation where you need increased cardiac output to send blood to your skeletal muscles, it's so that you can fight what is endangering you—or you can take flight and run away from that danger. The parasympathetic nervous system is responsible for restoring and digesting. It shunts blood to your stomach and increases your saliva to aid in the digestion of your food. When this system is activated, your immune system is supported.

Think about the kind of world we live in today. How are you prepared to win? There aren't any lions, tigers, or bears chasing you unless your office is in a national park or the African jungle. Instead, most of us find ourselves working in an office or at home, interacting with people instead of deadly animals. The interactions we engage in are more psychological than physical today. When you train weak, you are always kicking your SNS into overdrive and have unnecessary energy wasted on fears that really aren't posing any danger to you.

When you watch the news, you are on high alert. News used to be available to us for one hour a day. Today we are bombarded by news 24/7. If they were telling you stories on how to get better, it wouldn't be as catchy as them selling you a story of fear. As humans, we are wired to pay attention to anything that is a threat.

To be successful, you have to outlast and override these tendencies. You have to put more energy into your training so that when it comes time to perform, you are able to execute flawlessly—like a Navy SEAL. All of their suffering is in their training so that when it comes time to perform a task, there is no issue with that task being able to be accomplished.

One of the things I learned from working with Navy SEALS was how much time they spent restoring. You would think it would be all about doing more and more. But the only reasons they were able to do so much is because of the planning and preparation beforehand and the debriefing and learning that took place after.

What's more important than doing is who we are becoming. Take the time to reflect on who you are becoming. Take the time to prepare and plan so you go into a task with confidence. Take the time to assess so you can gain wisdom and understanding so that the next time you find yourself in a similar situation, you are able to navigate through it more seamlessly. When you see a professional, you see someone who isn't caught off guard. Professionals are cool, calm, and collected.

As impressive as you think Navy SEALs are, they are even more impressive when you speak to them in real life. I worked with a Navy SEAL for over a year. I wanted to train myself to be the toughest, hardest, most indestructible person out there. Mentally, I wanted to train like no one else, to be able to handle anything. I never wanted to be caught off-guard again.

What I didn't know is that I would be working on areas in my life that I had never explored before. I was examining my parents' relationship, comparing it to my relationship with my husband and going into some really dark places that I had never been before.

The thing about these darkest seasons is that the light can be even brighter. I had no idea what I would have to encounter and face off with. I was pregnant with our third child, and everything started to hit me really hard. She was going to be a girl, and I felt an enormous pressure on me to bring her into a perfect environment, an environment that I never had. I never wanted her to see her parents fight. I never wanted to give her that sick feeling in the pit of a child's stomach when they think something terrible is about to happen to their parents and that their whole world is about to crumble. I never had this with my two boys. Having this baby girl inside of me became something really personal.

I started looking at my mom and the decisions she made and wondered why she made those decisions. Why didn't she ever leave? What is that blank stare that some women have as they age where they just become hardened by life? It's the mom at home whose husband goes to work and she is in the house all day going crazy, cooking, cleaning, trying to take care of everyone but failing miserably to take care of herself. She starts to fall apart. She can grow more distant from her husband. She ends up eating more to soothe herself, and then all of a sudden, she becomes unrecognizable to herself, to her husband, even to her children. It's a form of self-betrayal.

We become short-tempered. For me, it would be me screaming at our children. I became my parents. I would say the things to them that my parents would say to me. I would hear myself and be mortified. At times, I could feel like I was my parents. The greatest thing about my training is that I became very self-aware and would catch myself doing it and stop it. Eventually you can feel the feelings rise up in you and stop it before it ever happens. You get to a place where you control the outcome by never allowing that weaker version to grow any longer.

I don't know if that has ever happened to you, but it's all quite scary. You become the thing you said you never would. Those moments when you have that out-of-body experience, you have a choice. Catch yourself. See it and change. Or continue to become someone else by default.

It takes courage to lead your life. It takes courage to change. It takes courage to admit what is wrong and get very real about correcting it.

I learned through spending time with myself that I could see what I was becoming and I could make a decision to change. It doesn't mean that I'm perfect, but it means that I am aware of myself. That is where all your power is. It takes courage to admit what you are doing wrong, to stop and to change direction.

As a wife. As a mother. As a business leader. I have gone way off, and it's those moments when we catch ourselves that we can choose to make a better version of ourselves. We stop tolerating whatever is happening and start to take action to change the outcome. We become like our Creator and become a creator of our very own lives.

I used to think that my parents failed me. I used to think that everyone who ever wronged me failed me. I used to think that my own family abandoned me and betrayed me. Even though they did horrible things to me—betrayal, extortion, abandonment, ambushes—all these things made me stronger in the end. When you become really real with yourself and the people around you, life starts to take a different direction. You tolerate less. You've already seen this before.

"Do what you came for, friend." (Matthew 26:50)

So many of us are living in superficial and fake relationships. On the outside, we appear to be so perfect and put together. On the inside, there is a brewing hell. To get to the place where we are functioning at optimal levels, we have to walk "through" our own hell.

Face. Confront. Admit to all the things about ourselves that we refuse to.

That little girl in me had to die. But we can't kill what we don't acknowledge exists. What's inside of you? For me, there was a lot of doubt.

When I was a student studying to be a doctor, I was working in a bank to pay my way through school. My aunt got me a job there the summer before I started university. This was before I had the major falling out with my father. I worked that summer with my aunt and did a good job. I was doing the inside operations of the cash management for the bank. It was pretty cool, seeing the inside workings of a bank, how the money is distributed and flows back in, every dollar accounted for.

When I worked in that bank, there was a VP I was able to spend some time with. She was a powerhouse in the bank. She had an office, and when she came in, everyone perked up. When she spoke, everyone listened. She had taken a small interest in me and spent some time with me and taught me a little bit about the business world. Looking back, I never even realized at the time who I was in the presence with. I just felt it.

I remember one day sitting in a room with the VP of the bank. She looked at me and told me something shocking: Everyone is replaceable. I thought to myself, *Well, that's not nice.* I have come to find out that business isn't about being nice.

She was right. Everyone is replaceable. Some are harder to replace than others. Sometimes you will need to find multiple people to do the job of one, but in the end, if you have a well-oiled machine of a business, you should be continuously attracting new talent that keeps everyone on their feet. When you have a great team, everyone knows this, and they are constantly working to better themselves so that they are incredibly difficult to replace.

Everyone should care about advancing the team so the team can continuously win. A company can't pay you more without you first doing more to make it more money. If you're not doing anything more and want to get paid more, that is called theft.

People steal from businesses all the time. They steal businesses' time, resources, and energy by not being fully engaged at work. They are on social media when they should be attending to clients. They are taking care of children at the expense of the business. That's why you have to put in more hours today and make yourself more available "after hours" or you will be replaced by someone else who will.

At the bank, because I was liked by the VP and did good work, I was offered an opportunity to join a special team of people who got paid very well going around and servicing the ATM machines throughout the entire Toronto area. This position was really only available to retired policemen and people with high security clearance because of all the money that was being handled.

That job was my saving grace while I was in school. I built a great relationship with my manager, and he would give me any and all the extra shifts that I could grab to pay my way through school. It was a 24/7 job. Three shifts. I would go to school in the morning and then work a double shift. After school, I would go to work from 3:30 to midnight and then pick up the midnight shift until 8:00 a.m. the following morning.

Sound familiar? That was exactly what my father used to do to make ends meet. I was never afraid of working. This is what makes me harder to be replaced. What makes you harder to be replaced? Do you even care to cultivate this? Or do you think, like most people today, that your workplace is lucky to have you? Everyone is replaceable. When you know this, you work differently. You have a higher level of regard and respect for the work you do and the way you do it. Your excellence at work will make your workplace value you more. It becomes a positive-feedback mechanism.

What happens when you don't value your work or the people you work with and want more for yourself? You become a wolf in sheep's clothing.

There was this older woman in the cash management team who had all these pictures of the Virgin Mary plastered on the wall of her cubicle. I remember her smell. She always smelled so nice. She spoke about her children like they were angels and talked about how hard they worked and how proud she was of them. When an ATM bank machine had a jam, we were the ones who were responsible for going to that site and fixing the jam.

The job would happen because the gears in the machine were getting worn out. A multimillion-dollar operation controlled by a two-cent plastic gear. We wouldn't ever fix the gear—we would throw it out and REPLACE it.

This is how some people are when you become dispensable to a business: It's more cost effective to just get rid of you than to fix you. That's why you can't allow yourself to get worn out. If you hem and haw about being overworked, just know that you are the easiest to replace. You complain because you don't value your work and your part in the giant machine.

The machine would jam up because of bad parts, but it would also jam up because of old or tattered money. If there was money with tape on it, had staples in it, or if it was too fragile, it would rip in the machine and cause a jam.

When we loaded the money in the cassettes, we had to "cull" or pull out the bad money to make sure that it wouldn't cause future jams. Certain branches of the bank always had jams in their machine because the tellers never loaded the money properly. They wouldn't take the time to line up the money nicely and pull the bad bills out. Their poor work ethic cost the banks millions when their machines shut down, and the customers would be pissed off when we would go to an ATM and it would say "Temporarily Out Of Service."

You start to see patterns in people's work habits after a long enough time. On Friday nights, the tellers were rushing out and doing bad work, and that would cause many jams for us to clear up on Saturday morning. Those workers pretended to care, but really, they were doing just enough to clock in and clock out so they could get paid.

Being on the inside operations of the bank allowed me to get a window into HOW people work. The branches with the most jams were often the messiest. If you went into their bathrooms, it was another disaster. You either care or you don't. Your level of care flows into every area of your work. Excellence pays attention to the details.

You have to look deeper than just the surface, though. Some people look so well-manicured on the outside when they are a disaster on the inside. They put more money into their makeup and hair products than they do in the development of their character.

The same woman who was so neat, tidy, and detailed, we had to bring all the "bad cash" to her. She was responsible for debiting and crediting the system with the replacement of the bad cash for the new cash so that every bank machine had a cash trail and every dollar was accounted for. I came to find out that she was creating new phantom accounts and stealing money from the bank. She stole millions. All the Virgin Marys in the world couldn't save her from being arrested. She was a wolf in sheep's clothing.

Learn to look more deeply into a person. Often what people are looking to portray about themselves is one big smoke screen.

Sometimes, we want so badly to believe in people. We think we can change people. We think because we value someone, they value us just as much. This isn't how it goes. Who you tolerate in your business matters. There has to be trust in a business, but there also have to be systems to verify that people are not abusing your trust. Trust but verify.

I later came to find out that assistant of mine was stealing from me on an ongoing basis. In one breath, she was sending me cards to say how much she valued me and how thankful she was for changing her life. In another breath, she was stealing from me, my business, and my family.

Not everyone or everything is as it seems. The best businesses understand this. If you have people who are exceptional, reward that. True trust is something that is really hard to find. And just because you have it for one year doesn't mean it's always yours. We have to constantly be earning and giving trust to those who surround us.

Work with those who deserve your attention. But remember change is really hard for people, and what you will come to find out is that the majority of people don't really change—they just become more of who they are. Do the work of carefully examining yourself, your past, and what values and beliefs were placed into you subconsciously by your parents. You can't change what you don't see.

CHAPTER 10

Don't Get Big and Stupid

T HE KEY TO longevity is to always have that "start-up" mentality. Sometimes becoming big can slow you down. Start-ups become successful and then stop taking risks, thinking big, and testing new theories. They change the way they approach everything once they hit a certain point on the growth chart.

Kodak is a classic example of this pitfall. In 1996, the company was at the top of its game with over 140,000 employees and a two hundred billion-dollar market cap. Cut to 2012: Kodak was bankrupt. Like other massive companies, Kodak refused to adapt to changing markets. When an employee invented the digital camera and presented it to the board, he was laughed out of the room. The company's leaders refused to see how the markets were changing, and they refused to change Kodak's identity. They paid the ultimate price. This old and slow thinking cost them their entire business.

My industry of insurance is very old and conservative. Not much has changed in hundreds of years. The people who are doing business the way it has always been done, however, are destined for failure.

We are constantly changing things up. I am constantly looking to cross-pollinate with other influencers in different industries to give us our edge.

You cannot be afraid to invest in your future. You cannot afford to be stagnant. In business, there is no such thing as maintaining. You are either growing or declining. This chapter will show you how to grow.

It's critical to never forget where you came from. We see this in politicians who get into politics to serve the people and then become career politicians who are working to keep their power and position at the expense of the people rather than remembering why they came into office in the first place—to help people. Power and greed take over. It stops being about the people and adding value, and it becomes a game of how-long-can-I-maintain-what-I-have.

Business is the same thing for most people, unfortunately. I believe that people want to become entrepreneurs because of an idea. Either you have an idea that you believe will help people tremendously, and you are willing to take a chance and risk your safety to make this idea come to light…or you just want to make a buck.

In the beginning days of business, there is a hustle that is in the air. It's the greatest feeling in the world. I had this feeling every time I would move to a different territory and have to start from scratch. When you have nothing to lose, you give it all that you have.

I remember working in New York. I lived in Long Island and drove into the city. I never wanted to take public transportation. There was something I loved about driving into the city and seeing the landscape before I entered the tunnel. It never got old.

I would wake up at 4:00 in the morning and be on the LIE by 5:00 or 6:00 a.m. The thing about New York is that you think you are getting a head start, and then you see everyone else is already ahead of you. The hunger is in the air in the form of red brake lights at 6:00 in the morning going into the city. I would leave home in the dark and come home in the dark. There was no time limit on what I was willing to put in to make my business a success. This is true for every territory I walked into. You might have been there longer, but I knew I was hungrier than you, and I knew it would just be a matter of time before I dominated you.

The truth is, every business needs a period of hunger like this to get off the ground. Starting a business requires ENORMOUS amounts of discipline and energy. Like a plane wanting to get in the sky, it uses the most fuel taking off. Once in the air, it gets more fuel-efficient. This is a great place to be when you are flying, and a very dangerous place to be when you are in business.

A lot of people at the "in-the-air" stage in the business take their hands off the wheel, go into autopilot, and even start taking naps. You should be paying attention and planning and preparing the next steps, or else you end up becoming very susceptible to attacks.

In special forces, they have something called "violence of action." This is when you attack hard and fast when the enemy is least expecting it. When businesses get big and comfy and are on autopilot, there couldn't be a better time to attack them.

These businesses get so used to doing what they have always done. They forget that there is a difference between having systems to help the business run versus doing the same thing over and over again because it worked in the past.

We see this in big business, where the same company that came into the market to disrupt the dinosaur has now become the dinosaur. They take forever to make a decision. They have a committee for the committee that's in charge of the committee to see if the committee is doing their job right. Everyone is in meetings all the time, and no one is working anymore. Everyone is inspecting and no one is innovating. Everyone is playing it safe, and no one is taking a chance on a new idea.

A lot of industries have very old people at the top. Bill Gates and Warren Buffet are exceptions. Unfortunately, in business there are a lot of people who take a chair and fall asleep at the wheel. They fail to lead the company because leading the company means that you are creating change.

Leading and managing are two very different things. It takes someone with a vision for the future, a vision for a better way, and the courage to execute on their vision to continue to lead a company. Most people in companies today are managing, not leading. They are managing their position so that no one takes their position. They are managing the value of the stock and timing it so when they are ready to retire, their payout is huge. Instead, they should be investing into the company and taking a short-term loss so that the company can reap a gain in the future.

A great example of this is Adobe predicting a loss to the shareholders so they could change their business model and be in business in the future, as opposed to playing it safe, showing a profit for the shareholders, and then filing for bankruptcy later on because they got swallowed by another company that wasn't afraid to invest.

At Amazon, there is something called a "Day 1 mentality." It's a mentality that ultimately should never die because it's what breathes life into the blood of the organization.

In my business, what has allowed us to continuously win has been our ability to think like a start-up all the time. Even when it may appear to others that we are losing, we know that we are winning because we are building. Never be discouraged when you are doing massive amounts of hard work and someone is ahead of you and not working as hard as you. If you are working on the right things, you have to know that it will pay off for yourself—and they will start to descend if they rest for too long.

The real question is: Can you train yourself to withstand the heat in the small dip so you can continue with the plan and come up victorious in the end? When you are starting in business, the energy is on your side. Everything is new and exciting. Every business can fall into a regular business cycle. Usually after the high comes the stagnation and then the low.

It doesn't have to be that way if you can constantly disrupt yourself.

Think about our pilot friend taking a nap while the plane is on autopilot. This is dangerous when done in business. What new thing are you working on? What if while the plane was flying in autopilot, the pilot was training and learning a new skill instead of taking a nap?

How many people would do that? The ones who are succeeding are. I did this year after year in my business, constantly testing out new ideas. I have started so many projects...and most have never taken off. The point is that you never stop testing out new ideas and never stop investing in what could be a game changer.

That's why entrepreneurs are so amazing—because they took the fall that many of us weren't willing to take. That's why we get paid so well when it finally catches—and catch it will. The whole point is to get as big as you possibly can and become the best leader you possibly can. That means having an enormous ability to influence, to create change, and to build. It doesn't matter how big you get; continue to grow, continue to push yourself, continue to disrupt and challenge yourself to get even bigger!

Don't operate from fear or complacency. What happens when you operate from fear? You don't make the right decisions. You start thinking in a way that leads you to make the wrong decision. Never make a decision from a low place or state. Get back to the light to change your state. Think about how you felt when you first started. Like a new relationship, that new love. You would do anything. You would risk anything. No matter how big you get or how long you have been in business, maintain that "Day 1 mentality."

CHAPTER 11

Family-Timing and Sequence Matters

I F I HAD a daughter, I would tell her, "Get your education. Get your career on track. And become the best at what you do before you even entertain the idea of having children."

It's the truth. Take advantage of not being tied down. Work your ass off when you are young and unattached. If you are a woman who thinks your career won't take a hit when you have kids, you have no idea what you are talking about. The order must be your career, then love/marriage, then kids. When you do choose to have a family, your family doesn't come first—it becomes your everything, and you have to learn how to integrate your family into everything you do and all that you are. Get things done in the right order. And as I've said, who you marry matters more than anything else, so choose wisely.

When you get married and then have kids, you learn how much time you really have. Having children and being in business is not easy. It's a constant war for your time, attention, and energy. You have to get both on the same team if you are going to succeed, or something will eventually give. You can't afford to let your family or your career die.

I have no idea why people think that not spending time with your family means you are not "choosing" them. Going to work and doing your job exceptionally well *is* choosing your family. We don't live in the factory age anymore. The opportunities to sow seeds of greatness within your family are not available with mediocre positions. You must work hard.

When a family has a child, more of the strain will go on the woman. You can sit there and chant, that's not fair. Life isn't fair. Get over it. Anyone saying otherwise has no idea what they are talking about. Does male breast tissue produce milk? No, I didn't think so. Nice try, though, for all of you applying for paternity leave. The mother is bonded differently to the newborn and needs to find the time to nurture that child in the first few years. One of the greatest decisions I made as a young woman was to work as hard as I possibly could so that when the time came to have children, I was more prepared to give to them.

I hear young people talking about having children so they can feel loved. Please don't.

Children take much more in the beginning than you think. Of all the luxuries I have experienced on earth, of all the rewards I have received, there is nothing more precious to me than being a mother, and the love I receive from our children is God's greatest gift to my life. But this high value gift comes with a very high cost of maintenance. It's absolutely worth it, but the reality is that no one really ever tells you how much it can leave you feeling depleted in the beginning because there is a lot of giving of yourself when you have children. In the beginning, it feels like you are giving so much. I've always said that you can never give what you don't have so make sure you take care of yourself first so you have more to give to your family.

Make sure that in the act of giving to your children that you are also receiving so that you don't feel empty. While children do take from us because they are so dependent upon us in the beginning, you must receive all the gifts that they give along the way as well. Be aware and feel the joy they bring to you with their smile, their laughter, their sweet scent, the softness of their voice.

Our children are the world's most prized investment. Like any investment, it will take many years of putting in. All those diapers, the strollers, the car seats—we often forget how much was done for us. Being a parent is a reminder of how much we must appreciate and honor our parents for giving as much as they could the best that they knew how to give in their time. When I was younger and naïve, I used to judge my parents, criticize their choices. The truth is no one is a perfect parent, but somehow they were perfectly chosen to be our parents, and we can learn from them if we find the deeper meaning in all the events that took place in our childhood.

This is not easy for people to stomach. Children initially require a massive deposit, but the return is infinite. In the beginning, it does feel like they take away so much. They take away your time, they take away your energy, they take away your money, they even take away your brain cells. Does that mean no one should have children? Absolutely not. There is no greater gift in the world. There is no greater miracle in the world. But timing is everything. I say this to you because so many women later on in their lives run the risk of feeling used and depleted if they don't learn how to replenish themselves and pour back into themselves along the way.

I didn't want my career to compete with my kids, so I waited until later to have them. Now, because I'm successful, I get to integrate my family life into my business life, not the other way around.

I hate when I hear people say "family first." What are you implying? When I choose to work that my family comes last? That you are so ethical and I am immoral? Or do you use that catchy slogan "family first" as an excuse as to why you lack results and motivation to do more with your life? Do you use your children as a reason to hide behind not working? Do you see how bad that sounds?

Let's get something straight—we live in a wacky, sometimes upside-down world. Everyone is chanting and marching for equality, and the truth is you are marching for something that has never and will never exist. It will never exist because the world needs us to be different. Our differences create life. Differences CREATE. The best relationships are not the ones where they are identical but complementary.

A great family is going to be made up of different personalities, but they are all united in values, principles, and a common mission. Households get divided when there is a lot of comparison and competing. Competing for time, energy, resources. I believe in roles. Everyone must do their part to the best of their ability. Instead of comparing what you do and what the other person is not doing, make sure you are all doing your part.

That's also how the best teams function. When you have a team where everyone is the same, that isn't a great team. My team is made up of so many different people. We come from different backgrounds, countries, cultures—our upbringings are all unique. Yet we are the same on the inside. We want to win, and we want to be around other people who want to win.

So just how does one manage to have a great family and a great business with a great team? What's worked for me is getting everyone and everything on the same page. My business doesn't compete for time with my family, and my family doesn't compete for time with my business. That's also true for everything that is important to me. I find a way to integrate all the things that matter in my life as opposed to having them compete for time and pulling me in many directions.

I'm fortunate to have my own business so I can incorporate my family in my work, but I see people manage this successfully even when they don't have their own business. Whatever you do, you have to give it your all. What does matter is that you time things as perfectly as you can because the sequence in which you do things does matter.

Remember that song we used to sing—*First comes love, then comes marriage, then comes the baby in the baby carriage?* What do you do when life works in a reverse order? The truth is if you mess the sequence up, it will be harder for you. Having a baby and trying to start a career at the same time is very hard. I see people attempt to do this in my business, and it absolutely affects them.

When you are young, work your butt off. Stop getting distracted. Plug in those twelve to sixteen hour days and make massive dents in your career. This is how you can accelerate your skills. This is how you launch yourself further than everyone else to create the space and time that you will need later on to make those deposits into the nurturing of your children or hiring all the necessary help that you need. I have a lot of help around me. All of my family lives in a different country, but there are a lot of people at work who help to fill in those gaps to keep this ship moving. If you are a woman, it is very different. A man having a child and working and a woman having a child and working are not the same.

Remember—it's not supposed to be the same. Keep reminding yourself of that. This equality thing is the greatest lie. It causes too much unnecessary tension when we are constantly comparing ourselves to people from whom we are designed to be different. When a woman delivers a baby, her body physiologically feels things that the man cannot and will not feel. Our hormones are different, so of course our feelings will be different.

I was the woman who walked into the hospital and told them I wanted to do everything natural, no epidural and no Pitocin; let everything happen "naturally." Listen, when things change, things have to change. My tune quickly changed when I realized that this pain was no joke. Some women can handle it and some cannot. I clearly needed an epidural. I made sure to get one for the birth of all of our other children as well.

This is the thing about life: We start out planning and preparing how everything is going to be, and then we have to make changes. It doesn't mean you are a failure. It means that you are human. You adapt, make changes, and keep moving.

I used to think that formula was evil. Why on earth would you give them formula when you can breastfeed? Again, things change. I did both, and there is nothing wrong with that. I'm grateful to have three healthy, beautiful children. No one has all the answers except God. Be careful how you judge others and especially how you judge yourself for changing your mind along the way. It's okay to make adjustments as you figure things out. Hopefully, you will be surrounded by people who are very patient with you and who know you have a lot on your plate and you are doing the best with what you have. That's why reading other people's stories helps us to understand that we are not alone. We can listen to what people have to say, but in the end, we have to make a decision to lead the outcome of our life—we must Stand Alone.

Having children has been one of the greatest blessings of my life. I had no idea I would love being pregnant and a mother as much as I do. I would have ten children if I could. I absolutely loved being pregnant. Some women hate it. We are all different.

As much as I love my children, there is no way I would have the success that I have if I messed up the sequence. Sequence matters. How you build matters. Just like an architect has a blueprint before they attempt to build a building, you need a blueprint for your life. That doesn't mean that you won't have to make adjustments along the way. As you are living your life, things will come up, but when you have something to compare it to, you can hold yourself accountable and get back on track.

I studied my whole childhood to be a doctor. When most children were watching cartoons, I loved reading chemistry books. Science has always fascinated me. From an early age, I was set on becoming a doctor of medicine. I did a lot of volunteering in a cardiac unit and a cancer center. I wanted to be a doctor to help people and to educate them. I have always been intrigued by gaining more knowledge. I love systems, and I enjoy learning how the body works. If there is a problem, thinking about where that problem is in the system and then finding the solution has always been enjoyable for me.

After I moved to the United States at twenty-five years old, I needed to make money. My dreams and plans of becoming a doctor got flipped upside down. I was put in a situation where survival outweighed what I had planned for my whole life. My blueprint needed to be put on hold.

When I was looking for a job, I called around for work in a lab because that was where I had experience and was what I was used to. The pay that they were offering wasn't going to cut it. There was no way I could survive on that level of income. I worked in a bank while I was paying my way through university, so I called around to work in a bank, and again, that pay wasn't going to cut it either.

Then I received a phone call from an insurance company and went to an interview. When they called me, they said that there was experience that I had that would work very well in their industry. I had no idea what they were talking about. I had no knowledge about insurance.

I was also called by a pharmaceutical company. I went to the interview for the pharmaceutical company first. It was in Nutley, New Jersey. The lady was impressed with my background and was interested in bringing me on board. I told her that I had one more interview to do and I would follow up with her.

When I went to the insurance interview, it was pouring rain that day. There was a man standing at the door, and he opened it for me. I sat in the lobby, waiting to be called. I went into a big room with a ton of books and a large desk. I was overwhelmed with the presence of the room. It smelled of success. It was a quick meeting, and I remember asking the interviewer, "Have you read all these books?" Then, they brought me into another room with a large American flag. I was so nervous that they were going to ask me to say the pledge of allegiance. I didn't know what it was, and I was so nervous. A gentleman came out. He was poised, confident, spoke in that strong New York/New Jersey accent, and explained the position in a group setting. I had no idea what was going on. I thought to myself, *How strange! In America, they do interviews in a group setting?*

I then met with another manager, the same manager who opened the door for me when I first walked into the building. At this point, there was so much information. All I could remember were all the books in the first room, the American flag in the second room, and the money that the other guy was saying that people made in the company.

When I sat in the room with the man who opened the door for me, there was something about him. He looked ultra-successful, but not in the way you may be thinking. He had confidence. He had a leather jacket on. His office looked more relaxed and comfortable. He was cool and confident. He looked like the kind of guy who wasn't trying to impress me, but he was very intriguing. He asked me the weirdest question: if my mother and father were both drowning in water, who would I save first and why?

I said neither. (I was *clearly* not in a good place with my parents at that time.)

He smiled at my answer. He didn't know anything about my situation at the time. At this time in my life, I was completely abandoned by both of my parents. I was navigating through everything without them. The answer sounds so harsh, but it was the truth at that time. That's what was so good about that interview with the guy who opened the door for me—it felt really real and raw. He didn't judge me for my answer; he was intrigued by it. He asked me what my plans were, and I told him that I wanted to be in his chair one day and have an office as well. And he said perfect, then I can go home and relax.

We instantly connected. This man changed my life. I wouldn't be who I am in the insurance industry if it weren't for him. His name is Barry Dillah. He was my manager for the first three years in the insurance industry and taught me so much about sales, leadership, working with people, and confidence.

Along my journey, I've always been blessed with people who added tremendous value to my life, and I only pray that I could add that same value back into the lives of others. That's what leadership is all about. That's what being an EXTRAORDINARY leader is all about: letting life serve you, learning through all your experiences, then serving the life of someone else through your story.

Family isn't first for me. It's my everything. The people who become my family through my journey mean the world to me. There's a saying that blood is thicker than water. When you look into where this saying comes from, you also find the saying, "The blood of the covenant is thicker than the water of the womb." This saying actually implies the opposite of what we are taught to believe about familial bonds. Most of us are raised to think that the family we are born into is more important than everything. When you become a leader and you realize that you don't have to manage the situation you were given, but you can actually create the life you want to live by picking and selecting the people you want to live with and be on a mission with, everything opens up. A blood covenant is created when you go to battle with and for people. The water of the womb has betrayed me more than I want to think about.

One of my favorite verses in the Bible that reminds me of this is *John 15:13*:

> *Greater love has no one than this: to lay down one's life for one's friends.*

Why not parents? Why not siblings? Why not children? Why friends? If you read the entire scripture, you will see there is a discussion of the vine and the branches. What are you a part of? What is feeding you?

When I joined the company, there was another manager under whom I was assigned. Her name was Laura Fisher. She was a gift from God to me at one of the hardest times in my life. She knew I didn't have any family that I was connected to at that time and would take it upon herself to invite me everywhere with her. If there was a holiday, she made sure that I was never alone. She became a like a sister to me. She taught me how to sell and showed me a path to follow as a producer in this company. I would go on to become a top producer for the entire company because of these two great people—Barry Dillah and Laura Fisher. Laura and I have gone through so much in this business—getting married and having children all while running a business. What a women goes through while she is running a business, raising children and doing her best to be a great wife, mother, and CEO is not something that is easy, and few people really understand the different energies and personalities that it takes to pull this one off. Being strong in the masculine space of business while maintaining the feminine side to nurture and love your family. It's rare and it will take you being OK with not everyone understanding you, but you will need to surround yourself with people who love you unconditionally to help you navigate through this.

I am very grateful for my team that allowed me the space to grow and evolve as a leader through all these years. When I think back to how I used to lead as a young individual versus now being a mother, it is very different. I always have been a very highly driven individual, and I still am. What I have learned is how to channel my energy in different capacities. I remember some men in the business would tell me to have children so that I could calm down. Oh boy, that's not what you say to someone on a mission. I can see how my overwhelming energy could drive someone off a cliff. But the truth about people who are powerful sources of energy is that you will create a culture around you that appreciates that energy and uses it to fuel their dreams. It absolutely will drive people out who are intimidated by it because it can be very overwhelming to someone who can't understand that you are pushing for you. It has nothing to do with them, but they stand to be a great recipient of what all that energy can create.

Remember, energy cannot be created or destroyed, it can only transfer from one form to another. When you try to make a high energy person do less—which is what a lot of people are doing in highly Westernized parts of the world to make other people who do less feel comfortable about themselves—you are attempting to destroy their energy. The problem with this is that energy cannot be destroyed. When you are highly driven and are you around people who can't understand you and make you feel like you have to lower who you are to meet with them, this will make you develop large amounts of resentment. You have to know who you really are and play your cards to the fullest of your capabilities. It's not anything on the outside that determines your success—not gender, not color. Even age is a tricky one. I see some people who are younger and wiser than those who have lived longer but failed to evaluate their life. It's what's inside. Inside of you, where all this energy resides, you have to package it up and spit it out in direct proportion to who you are, not someone else. If you were raised in bad situations that could have made a deposit of anger, take that high energy and transform it into good.

God needs people with courage and energy to do His work. We don't make good decisions from low energy states. When you are around high energy people, cherish them. If you are a high energy person, protect and guard yourself against those who attempt to deplete you of it and change you into someone you aren't.

The Stand Alone level is when you can take ANY energy that comes your way and channel it to let is serve you and serve this world.

The energy that I have for my business flows into the energy I have for my family. When people told me to have children so I could calm down, they had no idea that having children would fuel me up even more! I became driven on a whole new level. My purpose got deeper and my resolve became stronger than ever because knew I was living for so much more. All my actions are so focused, I waste less time, and I have fewer stupid conversations with people. I am not wasting time because I value it more than ever. It has helped me to become even more efficient and effective at what I do. I know that I have the eyes of my children on me, and I'm here to lead them by example.

That's the essence of leadership. We must lead ourselves first so that we can truly lead others. Otherwise, we are just barking orders at people. And after a while, people get sick of that. People look at their leaders and look how they handle themselves, how they handle tough situations, and want to be inspired by them!

The owner of the company that I joined when I first moved to the United States was Eric Giglione. He looked like money. He was inspiration on steroids to me. The first time he walked into the room,

I felt his power in his presence. The year that I was a top producer for his company, my interaction with him was minimal. He's the kind of guy who could walk into a room, say one sentence to you, and make more of an impact than someone who spent years with you. That's power. He had power lines that he would drop into my subconscious, and it wouldn't be until many years later that I would appreciate his genius.

I believe that there are levels to leadership. The strongest way to ensure your success is to be on a team of leaders who can develop you in different ways. There are people who can manage the business from the numbers and reporting aspect, there are people who are better at working with people, and then there are rare people that seem to have it all. They are smart and strategic. While you are playing checkers, they are playing chess, and they are seven moves ahead of you. They already know they are going to win. YOU even know that they are going to win. You are wise to keep these people very close to you. Don't try to compete with them. Instead, find a way to complete them. They are a power source in your life. They will be successful with or without you. It sounds harsh because it's true. You need them more than they need you. If both parties can learn to have a mutual respect for one another, that's where the magic happens.

We all know the saying, "Show me your friends and I will show you who you are." Our friends can help us create the life we want to live. I'm not talking about acquaintances. I'm talking about real friends. People you go through tremendous ups and downs with.

Many people will come and go in your life. That's okay. Focus on keeping the right ones in your life. Don't worry about the ones who leave you—maybe they are supposed to create the space for someone better. And when you find good people, do everything in your power to stay connected to greatness.

The Vine and the Branches

"I am the true vine, and my Father is the gardener. He cuts off every branch in me that bears no fruit, while every branch that does bear fruit he prunes so that it will be even more fruitful. You are already clean because of the word I have spoken to you. Remain in me, as I also remain in you. No branch can bear fruit by itself; it must remain in the vine. Neither can you bear fruit unless you remain in me.

"I am the vine; you are the branches. If you remain in me and I in you, you will bear much fruit; apart from me you can do nothing. If you do not remain in me, you are like a branch that is thrown away and withers; such branches are picked up, thrown into the fire and burned. If you remain in me and my words remain in you, ask whatever you wish, and it will be done for you. This is to my Father's glory, that you bear much fruit, showing yourselves to be my disciples.

"As the Father has loved me, so have I loved you. Now remain in my love. If you keep my commands, you will remain in my love, just as I have kept my Father's commands and remain in his love. I have told you this so that my joy may be in you and that your joy may be complete. My command is this: Love each other as I have loved you. Greater love has no one than this: to lay down one's life for one's friends. You are my friends if you do what I command. I no longer call you servants, because a servant does not know his master's business. Instead, I have called you friends, for everything that I learned

from my Father I have made known to you. You did not choose me, but I chose you and appointed you so that you might go and bear fruit—fruit that will last—and so that whatever you ask in my name the Father will give you. This is my command: Love each other."4

4 *Holy Bible, New International Version.* (Biblica, Inc., 1973), John 15, BibleGateway, https://www.biblegateway.com/passage/?search=John%2015&version=NIV#fen-NIV-26702a.

CHAPTER 12

See with Your Brain, Not with Your Eyes

L EARN TO CONTROL what you see in order to understand what's really going on in a situation. Stop being superficial. Things are not always as they seem. There is something to be said for experience. An experienced individual sees what's happening very differently than someone encountering a situation for the first time. This is why who you surround yourself with matters so much.

When we are new to an idea or situation, there is so much that we could be missing. It's important to have the right people around us—people who can help coach and guide us. Think about *why* someone is telling you what they are telling you; it may open up your perspective.

Communication is more than just words. Words only make up 7 percent of communication, so an untrained individual will listen to what everyone is saying, while a trained professional will scan the overall picture. He or she will study a person's energy and look at body language, tone, volume, and stance. It pays to have an outside perspective as well. Sometimes, when we are in the midst of something, it's hard to see everything that is going on, but a person looking in from the outside has a clearer perspective. This chapter will show you how to see with your brain, get a new perspective, and learn how to read people, no matter what they are saying.

Go deep. Everyone today is living on the surface. In the last chapter, we talked about having a blueprint for your life. The reality is, you will have to change and make adjustments to your blueprint.

Work on your foundation. Work on being a person of principles and value. Your principles and what you value will help to guide you in the pursuit of whatever you are on a mission for. So, what are you on a mission for? What is your campaign?

The drug companies are on a campaign to sell you more drugs. That's why they spend an enormous amount of money advertising to you. In 2020, the pharmaceutical industry in the United States spent **6.58 billion US dollars** on direct-to-consumer advertising.[5]

How much does the food industry spend to get you to eat what they are making? How much does the consumer industry spend on endorsements to get you to buy what they are selling? Do you think it's a coincidence that you "feel" like eating something after you listen to commercials on television and radio and constantly see billboards suggesting to you?

Things don't just happen. Things happen just. They happen for a reason—find that reason. When you see that everything happens for a reason, you can get more intentional about your life. You can start to create the outcome you want to experience rather than just manage the circumstances of your life.

Go deep into this. I mean really dive into it. How much do you invest in your success? I have read almost every book on personal

---

[5]   "Direct-to-consumer spending of the pharmaceutical industry in the United States from 2012 to 2020," Statista, April 2021, https://www.statista.com/statistics/686906/pharma-ad-spend-usa/.

development that I could get my hands on when I joined the insurance industry. I knew nothing about sales, influence, marketing, or business. I went on a campaign to learn all that I could so I could apply it to my business and win.

How are you going to win if you don't armor yourself with ammunition and train yourself with the skills and information needed to execute?

The truth is you can't. All the industries that are on a campaign to own you end up owning you. Your body isn't what it should be. Your health isn't what it should be. Your financial state isn't where it should be. Your mental state isn't where it should be. And it's all because you are not controlling the dialogue. You aren't on a campaign to control and lead your life, so you are being led by default. Life is happening to you instead of you directing and leading your own life.

Learn about communication. What do you communicate to yourself? The words we speak are a small fraction of communication. Over 90 percent of communication is nonverbal: how we carry ourselves, how we dress, how well we take care of ourselves. Maybe you work at Google and you are a billionaire like Mark Zuckerberg, so you can wear jeans, a T-shirt, and flip-flops to work. My industry won't tolerate that.

What is your industry? Do you dress for it? Do you represent it? Do you speak its language? Do you speak the language of your customer? All these things make a difference in the level of success you are able to achieve.

We have people who come in for interviews wearing casual clothes. Their hair is a mess and maybe pink or blue. They have piercings. No effort was put into their outward appearance. What happened to "dress to impress?" Who are you impressing? Yourself? What are you communicating to your employer, to the company, to the customer? Do you care about them, or do you just care about your own personal "self-expression?" What does that say about you? That you are creative…or that you lack common sense and don't care about what anyone thinks except yourself?

Here's a newsflash: No company wants anything to do with that. A company hires you and is wondering, how hard will you work for me? Are you coachable? What is your intelligence level? What is your capacity to learn, adapt, and grow? How much value can you add to my company?

No company is hiring you so that you can "find yourself" on their dime. They hired you to produce results. Never get that confused.

How do you gain an advantage over everyone else? You think deeper and add more value than anyone else. Stop thinking about just yourself for a moment and start to really think about the bigger picture.

Mature yourself. When you are young and naïve, you care about expressing yourself, and you sometimes express yourself at the expense of others. The truth about business and life is that you have to think about others. You have to see how you fit into the bigger picture.

No one person is responsible for anything on their own. It takes working with many people at all different levels to make things work successfully. The greatest teams are made up of people who really care about more than just themselves. They care about the big picture, the mission.

So what investment are you willing to make into yourself so that you can win? I mean, *really* win? Stop living your life on default. The only way to override the campaigns that others have on you is with massive action on what you want to do and achieve for yourself.

The most important person you communicate with is yourself. Do you schedule time to think? Or is your time fractured and swallowed by social media, television, and the news? Are you so busy watching other people's opinions that you don't even know what yours is? Make a decision today to Stand Alone and control the dialogue in your life. Get around positive circles of influence that can add tremendous value to your life and make sure you contribute value back in the form of massive deposits into whatever you are taking withdrawals from.

CHAPTER 13

Spot an Ambush
and Walk Away

T HERE IS NOTHING worse than seeing someone walk right into an ambush completely blind with no idea what's about to happen to them. Don't be this person.

Part of winning in business is protecting yourself against unnecessary losses. I came into business with the same mindset as when I grew up: Everyone is equal, everyone wants what's best for their colleagues, and we are all in this together. I thought mine was an industry where we all raised each other up. As a female in a very heavily masculine space, I was able to rise through the ranks and build an empire of strong men and women. I thought people would be happy for me. I was able to rise to a level that no female had ever achieved in the seventy-plus years of the history of the company.

Boy, was I wrong.

After a particularly good year, my team went to a convention to celebrate our success. It was at the welcome reception that everything got really dark. People from other teams were screaming that evening,

"Shut that bitch up!" People ridiculed us. They called us losers and screamed obscene things about me. They got into my team's face, chanted nasty things, and did everything in their power to provoke us all. They waited for us to react, and then they turned on the cameras and labeled us as the demons that night. It was a complete mess. The same people I admired in the business detested us and with enough alcohol, the truth came out. I watched every member of my team walk onstage and—instead of being treated with respect—be ridiculed. What I learned is that people will help you as long as you don't come near them or take their shine away. As soon as that happens, you are marked as an enemy. They will make it a point to tarnish your image.

This chapter will show you how to navigate those challenges.

> *"Beware of false prophets, which come to you in sheep's clothing, but inwardly they are ravening wolves." (Matthew 7:15, KJV)*

What do you do when your hero becomes your enemy?

Elon Musk and the creation of SpaceX wasn't met with open arms. Neil Armstrong and Cart Eugene Cernan (astronaut and former Apollo 17 commander) testified and attempted to block commercial spaceflight and the way that Elon was developing his model. The same people he looked up to who had inspired him to push the envelope were throwing stones at him and attempting to halt his progress.

Why does this happen? Why is it so hard to celebrate someone else's success? Do we feel like they are taking something from us in their pursuit for more?

I made a decision when I moved from New York to Chicago that I would stop competing with everyone and that I would instead conquer. I knew I had to conquer myself and the business and not worry about competing with anyone ever again. I was working on conquering the business so nothing else or no one else would ever be in control of my results again but me. When you go to conquer something, you make your competition irrelevant. I never again wanted to put myself or anyone I led in a position to be vulnerable to attack.

The attack I experienced in New York was on resources. When you are dependent on anyone in business, you don't really have a business. I tell people this all the time in sales: If you don't know how to hunt—meaning if you don't know how to prospect—you really aren't good at sales. You aren't even in sales. You are an order taker. Finding and creating customers is a part of being in business.

If you are a doctor, a plumber, an accountant, a real estate agent, or in insurance, you can bet that you will go out of business if you can't prospect. In today's world, like with so many other things, people are getting weaker. They don't go above and beyond the call of duty. For the most part, people are doing the minimum and expecting the maximum in return. Their work ethic is terrible.

Being an entrepreneur is a blessing because you are in control—but only if you are in control. If you apply a nine-to-five, average mentality to entrepreneurship, you can be sure that you will fail and be replaced by someone who is willing to outwork, outthink, and outlast you. It takes stamina to start a business, be in business, and stay in business.

Work is a blessing in your life. It will give you purpose. It can help to transform you if it is challenging enough. A body in motion stays in motion. A body at rest stays at rest.

My son asked me one morning, "How does school help you make money?" A lot of people think they don't have to go to school because it's the cool and popular thing to say. But I would caution you against walking down that path. The person who is saying this to shrug off any and all responsibility isn't going to do well in the business world, either. School helps you to grow in structure and discipline, like how you need to wake up in the morning to go somewhere versus waking up in the morning because you feel like it. It helps to mature you as you have duties and responsibilities that you have to keep and complete.

Recently, I decided to homeschool our children to give them an advantage. I can control the curriculum. We travel a lot, so they can learn at an accelerated pace and have the time to travel and gain exposure to seeing and doing things with our family as opposed to racking up absences. I've been hearing lately of some very damaging ideas being taught in the school system. It used to be that you could send your kids to a private school and get a better education. I've come to realize that the state of the teacher's mind can and will affect and infect your children. Remember the verse about the vine. Teachers are a major source of nourishment to our children. What are *their* values? What are the values that they will transfer to our children? Do they hold themselves accountable to a higher level? Is discipline being taught in the school system today, or has discipline been removed?

As a parent, I want to be in charge of setting the values of our children. I want them to know how important God is. Why and when did this become such a bad thing?

So to answer my child's question: School will help to instill you with the work ethic and principles to apply to the real world to make money. School is practice. When you enter the real world—it's SHOWTIME. And you will play like you practice.

In 2015, I was working with Eric Thomas, the motivational speaker, author, and pastor. He came to our office and not only spoke to my team, but he spoke to my heart. What impressed me about him so much was how real he was. He wasn't pretending to be someone he was not. He was very real with who he was, and he never let his fame or popularity get to him. His life was about living his calling. I know his calling is bestowed to him from a much higher place. It shows up in how much he puts into working with children and communities.

I had the honor and blessing of doing some work with him in the past. I did a series with him at Michigan University and opened up for him in my hometown of Toronto, Canada. Both times, I knew I was training under a master. His voice has the ability to penetrate deeper than most. That's why people love him.

To this day, I still have people reaching out to me from that classroom in Michigan University saying thank you:

> *Hey Sabrina,*
>
> *Just sending you a quick message to let you know your talk on Eric Thomas's Success Series CD, School Vs. The Real World, has had an enormous impact on me to push my limits in my career and start my own entrepreneurial and self-development journey. I listened to it first five years ago and it still lives in my head.*
>
> *Hope you're doing well, continue to inspire, and are happy finding this message.*
>
> *Jake*

I have people who were in that classroom with me that I still keep in touch with. I follow them on social media and see they are leaders in their communities. I have another student who sent me a copy of her book and said that I inspired her to write. The truth is, they really do inspire me and feed back into me that nothing we do is insignificant. We are training and preparing for our future.

Our power comes from our preparation.

> *"We don't rise to the level of our expectations, we fall to the level of our training."*
>
> *—Archilochus*

In the past, if you had to learn a trade of a skill, you would become an apprentice.

If you want to learn a trade or a skill today, you have so many ways to learn. YouTube, virtual seminars…you can even take courses at accredited universities and learn from the top professors. I have done this. I have enrolled in courses from Harvard Business School and learned from the best professors. What I have come to understand is that my learning experience is so much richer because I have a real business to apply the lessons to directly.

Being a student is my super skill. I can study, model, and research things at a level much deeper than most. But there is something about the real world where studying is not enough. There is no substitute for real-world experience. My experiences in business have taught me in seconds what no course or business could have. My ability to learn and the gift of having real-life experience is what creates my success. When I say real-life experience, I'm not really talking about the good times. There are things that I have experienced in business that are eye opening. My studies have taught me that these things happen to everyone in business.

> *"If the world hates you, keep in mind that it hated me first. If you belonged to the world, it would love you as its own. As it is, you do not belong to the world, but I have chosen you out of the world. That is why the world hates you. Remember what I told you: 'A servant is not greater than his master.' If they persecuted me, they will persecute you also." (John 15: 18–20)*

When I was in New York and was being set up by the public relations team and painted in a bad light to the company, the people higher up in the company couldn't see what I was working on. I was always training my team at a higher level, teaching them to go above and beyond the call of duty. Thinking, *How can we offer more service to the groups that we worked with?* The PR team did not like this at all. They thought I was competing with them. I got ambushed. They made up stories about me to create unnecessary trouble. Being in New York was like an apprenticeship for Chicago. I tried to stand up for myself, and it was falling on deaf ears. I ended up walking away.

When I came to Chicago, I wanted to build on my experience. I never wanted to place my team in a position to be ambushed like that again.

Not everyone wants you to be successful. Not everyone is your friend. I know what it feels like to have someone smile in your face and stab you behind your back. I've made verbal agreements with people and thought because my word is gold, theirs would be too. This is not the case. Put things in writing. Trust, but verify. People change, and when circumstances change, the weak start to change their tune. That's the real and raw truth of business.

In Chicago, we got off completely from the lead system. The first ever in the seventy-year history of our business. The above-average training that I was giving my agents in New York continued into Chicago, and we now build the best relationships with the businesses that work with us. Our training is intense and ongoing. We hold everyone on our team to an incredibly high standard, and that results in great relationships and referrals for us.

That doesn't mean everyone loves us. Sometimes the hate can't help but to rear its ugly head if you don't kill it dead. Hate is a real thing. You will really feel it come on when you are doing what most cannot. Instead of someone learning from you and celebrating your success, it's easy for someone to justify where they are by finding something they hate in you so they can be OK with themselves.

It's no secret that there are very few women in leadership positions. This is true in many businesses across many industries. There are a lot of female artists and talent, but there are few in ownership and leadership roles. In the music industry, there are a lot of skilled artists, but very few own the record label. In the restaurant business, there are many great and talented chefs, but very few women who own the restaurant.

The world needs more women in leadership—but be prepared for what you will encounter. After you escape one ambush, there will be another. The more prepared you are, the less affected you will be.

There are many successful women in sales and women who are top producers in my industry, but there are very few women who make it up the ranks of leadership and are respected enough to have a seat at the table where their opinion actually matters.

My industry is heavily dominated by men. That's not a bad thing—it's just a thing. There has never been a woman in leadership who has had a team of my size and strength. I work and lead the toughest and most skilled men and women in the industry.

There was one year where we completely dominated on an international scale. If there was an award, we won it. If there was a first-place spot, we took it. I was never prouder of what we accomplished as a group. This immediately followed our being recognized in the previous year as the Agency of the Year and me becoming the first woman SGA of the year in the company's seventy-year history. You would think an accomplishment of this nature would be met with the utmost respect and honor....

Nothing could be farther from the truth.

I was so happy for the accomplishment of our team! We had team jerseys made. I rented out the top floor to hand the jerseys out as a thank you to everyone for all their hard work. We did our cheers together and got ready to join everyone else to celebrate as one company.

When we went to the welcome reception, we were greeted in a very unusual manner. Listen, salespeople are territorial. We are highly ambitious people who all like to win. I get that. I LOVE that. But I was not prepared for what was about to happen.

I wanted to take my team to meet with the CEO of the company and take a picture with him. We walked as a team. The stares, the glares, the hate—you could feel it. I was so happy for my team that I didn't pay much attention to it.

After dinner—and after a few drinks—the truth serum was activated, and the truth was released.

"Tell that bitch to shut up."

"It's about time someone told Sabrina to shut the f*$! up."

I couldn't believe the level of hate we were met with. Someone smashed a bottle of alcohol and threatened someone on my team. Then a fight broke out.

If you've ever watched a movie where everything slows down and you are taking all the information in slow motion—all the faces, all the words—it was like that, and it's forever etched into my mind.

I don't drink. I didn't have one drink that night. I was the most sober and awake person there. Everyone kept telling me to separate from my team. People high up in the company were approached, and they saw what happened and who instigated the whole thing. At one point, there was a manager and a top producer and his wife from another team screaming obscenities in the face of our team.

I looked at another manager and said to her, "What is going on here?"

This woman was screaming at me and my team. I went to her and told her to control herself. I looked at a manager I knew from that team and told her to tell her people to knock it off. She gave me the most cold and empty stare.

I knew I had to get my team away from all of that. We were getting everyone to go upstairs where we initially met that night.

I remember having the team all go up the escalator to get away from these people. After someone made a comment to me again, I saw people start to take their cameras out to record what was happening. If this ever happened today, the whole thing would have been recorded from the beginning, and it would have been on Instagram Live. I remember watching the people recording and wondering if they were recording the whole time or just after they screamed obscenities at us and made physical contact. It was a complete ambush that conveniently got recorded when my husband was defending his wife and our team.

The next morning, we had breakfast with the CEO in his room along with the other members of the company. I felt like I was waking up and that the night before had been one big dream that never happened. That day, I had to meet with the corporate counsel. An independent law firm was also contacted to come interview me and my team when we all got back. It was a series of ambushes. One after another.

I remember walking around that night by myself, and I remember every single person who came up to me and tried to lecture me, giving me glares and their opinions regarding what they thought had happened. I remember the people who claimed to be my friends hiding because they wanted to stay clear of this mess.

In the wild, female elephants are called matriarchs. The matriarch is the one that leads the herd because of her experience...but also because of her memory. These matriarchs build up a strong memory over time that allows them to remember friends and enemies. They can also remember places where the herd has found food and water in the past.

I will never forget the events of that night. I will never forget the faces of the people and the words that were spoken. I will never forget the hate that filled the entire hotel.

The next day was the awards ceremony. We collected our trophies, and as people continued to heckle from the crowd, I remembered thinking, *This too shall pass.*

The truth is, it's still inside of me. Just like every situation you have been through, it can make you or it can destroy you. I chose at that moment to take in what was happening and come to terms with the reality that this is business.

Everyone likes you until you become a threat. Everyone loves to cheer you on as long as you are beneath them. It's human nature.

I looked at people in my company when I first joined like they were gods. I admired them so much. I had so much respect for them and what they created—and I still do.

When you watch Elon Musk being asked how it feels to be attacked by his hero, his eyes water and his lips start to tremble. That's what makes greatness. We take those emotions and they fuel us to keep going, to get better, to do more.

I wish I could tell you the hate eventually stops. I really think it just morphs into different forms. Beware of the wolves that are dressed in sheep's clothing in your life. It's not the ones who state they are your enemy that you have to be concerned with. It's the ones who smile in your face and scheme and plot behind your back that you have to be more aware of.

If you think everyone is there to help you and everyone wishes you well, you really haven't been in business long enough. Eric Giglione taught me that you haven't made it UNTIL you have been sued. Since the beginning of time, we have stories of brothers killing one another, wars, conquests, and empires falling. From Cain and Abel, Saul and David, to WWII, and every battle fought after…we need to understand and learn from the past and, hopefully, you can be the kind of leader that remembers so you can avoid future landmines.

History tried to repeat itself with the PR team trying to create another smear campaign against my team in Chicago. This time, I didn't back down. I knew this was so wrong. It was being told to a union president that my team and I were responsible for the bad customer service of their entire group and that I was being removed from being able to service them. I didn't even work with that group anymore. When I went to confirm this information, it was exposed that it was all one big lie at our expense.

Let me tell you about why you need courage to stand up for what is right: It may seem insignificant at the time, but when you allow other people to slander your name so they can gain an advantage and you don't stand up for yourself, that behavior will come back to haunt either you or someone else.

As a leader, you must stand up for your people. What are you there for if you can't do that?

I wasn't OK with being attacked by the company anymore. Attacks come in different forms. Business is war without the swords and guns. They attack your character to make an attempt for you to bleed out. They want you to give up. The enemy wins when you fall back. Don't ever fall back.

You see this in the political world all the time. People attack people and their character, sometimes making up lies, because if they can get you to make that association with that person, they have damaged you in their eyes.

When people attempt to damage you and your reputation, stand up. Fight back. Good must prevail. Good must be strong and act with courage. Good must be louder. Evil will fill the void where there is no good and nature abhors a vacuum.

> *"Haters are confused admirers who can't understand why everybody else likes you."*
>
> —*Paulo Coelho*

The only way to fight against evil is with good. The right thing all the time. Stand up for what is right no matter the cost. When people manipulate the truth they paint you in a light that is not accurate. Use that energy that they are giving to you and flip it for good. Energy is energy. Take it and use it in the service of your greater mission. Do not get distracted, and do not allow it to throw you off track. The enemy has to confuse you and distract you to own you. Don't let them take up space in your head. Do what's right—because good always wins. Stay on the side of good by never compromising your values and principles.

What I have come to learn over time is that we will face many ambushes in our lives—some major like a major disease, an unexpected death of a loved one, the loss of a profound relationship—and some minor where it affects us but we come to terms with it more quickly. If I learned anything about leadership through the life of Jesus, it is that even the best of us are not always met with open arms. What's important is that we learn to control our emotions and stay focused on the bigger picture, and don't get distracted from your calling, mission, or purpose. We are all called to perform at a higher level. The major events of our lives can come to serve us and ultimately *prepare* us to handle more later on if we will make a decision to keep moving forward and focus on what is good and right. When we are in the darkest moments, it becomes vital that we make a decision to walk toward the light. Never make decisions in the dark (this is why training is so important so our instincts in those moments minimize damage) and move as fast as possible toward the light and surround yourselves with people that love you perfectly.

Remember, this too shall pass. The right relationships will come back to one another. We can learn from death and disaster and grow from it rather than getting destroyed by it.

CHAPTER 14

Staying Sharp

ALWAYS CHECK IN on and upgrade your environment. It's very rare for the people who start with you to be the ones who finish with you. The only people who should be able to finish with you are the ones who are not afraid to get uncomfortable and grow with you and your organization.

Unfortunately, entitlement is real. And while you can be loyal, when you are loyal to people who are no longer loyal to you, only you suffer. Check in with your team to really see how they are doing. Length of service, while important, isn't everything.

In sales, you are taught very early that you are only as good as your last week. Everyone needs to understand this in business. You must remain relevant or you will be forgotten.

This book has shown you how to become dangerous—and this chapter shows you how to stay that way. I will show you how to stay on your toes and conduct regular check-ins to make sure you, your team, your approach, and your partners—people who you entrust with more—are not becoming complacent and entitled. The closest people around you can turn against you. It happens. It's sad, and it hurts like hell. You will wonder how someone who once would have sacrificed so much is now sacrificing it all for self-gain.

I will show you how to continuously sharpen yourself. Never let your blade become dull. Surround yourself with people who aren't afraid to tell you the way things are. The TRUTH. Get away from people who just tell you pleasantries and try to keep you happy. This is death by a thousand paper cuts. They're so slight that you don't even feel them until the volume eventually causes you to bleed out. Remember that charm is the tool of the devil. Get to the truth in every conversation you have. Know the truth before you even ask any questions and see what the person you are confronting will do.

I would rather deal with the ugliest truth than the prettiest lie. When you are asking someone what the truth is, you should have already done your homework and spoken to multiple sources. When you find out, test your team. Will they tell you the truth or will they lie to you to save face? Anyone who is willing to lie to you and compromise the integrity of the organization to save face is a major liability. You may think it's no big deal and that people lie all the time. Be careful what you accept in your life to be normal. A business that fails to operate on clearly defined boundaries is not a business. You won't be in business for long. If you find someone doing things that are against the confines of what is acceptable in the business, you have an obligation to deal with this. If you ignore it, you are making a conscious decision to grow this.

This will be the hardest to do when it's the people you trusted the most who betray you.

I want you to be OK with being uncomfortable. Don't become complacent once you achieve success. Continue to push yourself and do what others won't. Physically, mentally, and spiritually, you need to be stronger than everyone else around you. You can't afford to have a weak area in your life.

Success—in business and in life—demands all of you, not just a part of you. How you are physically affects how you are mentally and emotionally. It's all connected. There are no days off from being at the top of your game. In this chapter, I go over what it takes to strengthen yourself mentally, as well as physically and spiritually.

The world demands all of you. There is no shortcut. There is no "one thing." And there definitely isn't a "hack." What there is is wisdom. Wisdom and the truth that stands the test of time. That's why—no offense—but if you are young and made your first million, no one should care. What we should care about is the next million and the million after that. If you lost it, did you get it back and grow it to become even more?

Anyone can be given something. There is a very big difference in the person who you become when someone is giving you something versus when you earn it. And when you earn something, it means that even if you lose it, you can get it back again. Because you earned it in the first place, you can do it again! The respect comes from what you DO with what is given to you. Do you go through life and continue to grow, or do you let everything that happens to you destroy you?

That's what I see. I have worked with tens of thousands of people in my seventeen years of business and the truth is, I still feel like an amateur. I feel like I have so much more to live and experience. I am constantly sharpening my skills and allowing myself to be fine-tuned by life.

I like nice cars. I have a lot of very nice cars. I've learned one thing that's really stuck with me about high-end cars—and that's that they need to be driven. If you push a Toyota to its limits, you may very well break it. But a Ferrari needs to be driven. If it isn't, it loses its ability.

So what are you? A Toyota or a Ferrari? What happens when someone pushes you to the edge of your existence and beyond? Do you need to be driven hard? Do you like the idea of being in a high-performance atmosphere? Do you like the idea of being surrounded by people who can tell you what you need to hear and not by people feeding and stroking your ego because you are sensitive and insecure? Someone telling you what you want to hear is manipulating you. Someone telling you what you need to hear is GROWING you.

Every human being has insecurities and fears. The point is to challenge them. The point is to train hard and create a stronger version of yourself. How we came into this world is not how we are supposed to exit. Life is working to strengthen us so that we can make deposits into the following generations. That's how you make an impact on your family, your company, your country.

In the end, I can't wait to hear my Father say those precious words to me: *"Well done, good and faithful servant! You have been faithful with a few things; I will put you in charge of many things. Come and share your master's happiness!" (Matthew 25:23)*

This lifetime could all be just one big test. Make sure you pass all the little tests along the way.

Stand Alone and commit to passing each test that life will throw your way. As you train harder than anyone else you will be better prepared than anyone else. Then you can EXECUTE like NO ONE ELSE.

Letter to My Unborn Daughter

M Y BOOK ENDS with a letter to my unborn daughter. I have a calling to make a positive impact on women and to help them realize their strength within. Too often, I see women in business who are unsure of themselves, and sometimes they just lack the support they need to feel comfortable enough to be strong. I want to be the person who encourages them to be strong, just like men are raised to be. I want to encourage them to own being a woman, to be proud of being a woman. I have always said that I would love the opportunity to raise a daughter and teach her from the beginning how to be a leader. I would want her to lead her life by example, and I would want nothing more to live to see her become a world leader.

The purpose of the book is not to be unkind, unfeeling, or mean but to show people how to remain tough, move through the darkest moments, and always find your way back to the light in order to win in the brutal game of business and, ultimately, life. In the end, you have to see yourself as the controller of the game, otherwise it will engulf and damage you. Know your strength within and rise above it.

"See to it, then, that the light within you is not darkness. Therefore, if your whole body is full of light, and no part of it dark, it will be just as full of light as when a lamp shines its light on you." (Luke 11:35–36)

Standing Alone is about not being afraid to be in the dark. Those dark times in our lives are when we are the most vulnerable and scared. It doesn't matter how much darkness is on the outside; I challenge you to Stand Alone and refuse to let any of that darkness inside of you. As leaders of this world we must be filled with light. And our light will help to guide those who follow us. You can be a great leader wherever you are. In school, at home, at work, in business, in sports, in the political arena—we are all called to bring our light.

One of the things I am most proud of in my life is my deep relationship with God. I don't know if I'm religious or spiritual, but I am very proud to say that I am a Christian. While I was in university studying to be a doctor, I decided to also major in religion. What better way to understand why people think the way they think and to understand why people believe what they believe?

I studied all the world religions. It was fascinating to me. One hour I would be in biology class and they would be mocking people who believed in God. The next hour I would be in a course on Judaism studying the work of Moses Maimonides.

There is something to be said about having the ability to hold two diametrically opposed ideas in your head at the same time. This, I believe, is an art—an art that is very much lost today.

Studying world religions didn't make me less of a Christian—it made me a stronger one. Taking courses and having deep conversations with atheists didn't make me an unbeliever. In fact, it did the opposite: It made me a better and stronger believer because I had the chance to challenge my ideas.

So many people today are lost because they aren't taking the time to see things through, commit, ask good questions, and listen to what other people have to say, especially others with opposing views.

Everything I ever went through was preparing me to excel in the business world. Every hardship, every betrayal, every disaster—instead of destroying me, it was preparing me to handle more than I could have ever imagined in the future.

Don't get caught up in comparing yourself to others.

"Do not despise these small beginnings, for the Lord rejoices to see the work begin." (Zechariah 4:10, NLT)

Where you are and what you are going through is exactly what's supposed to happen. Take the time to do it all well. Learn from everything.

A few years back, I decided to hire the Navy SEAL David Goggins to train me to handle more, to sharpen my mind like never before. What I didn't know was how much I would grow spiritually as a result of our conversations. I wanted to examine my thoughts and see if my thinking was on par with our world's greatest warriors. I had just given birth to two boys. I felt like there was something else that I was needing in my life, and I had no idea what that was. I had the best conversations with him. Who would have thought that hiring someone to make me "harder" could actually work on making me a better human being? In our first sessions, he asked me to start writing and just begin to examine my past, my childhood, and to look into it all on a deeper level. I wanted nothing to do with this. I avoided it. I avoided him. The very things we are looking to avoid are the very things that we need to confront to go to the next level of our lives. Well, he won that battle…I started writing about the things that were lodged in the deepest parts of me. During this time while working with him in August of 2018, I felt compelled to write a letter to my unborn daughter. Later that night, I took a pregnancy test and found out I was pregnant. There are times in my life where God taps me on my shoulder and reminds me that everything will be OK. This was one of those moments for me. I don't believe in coincidences. I believe that everything happens for a reason. We may not understand it all at the time, but when we look back, we will see how it all comes together like a beautiful masterpiece.

As I was writing about my childhood, I was examining a lot of very hurtful things I went through as a child…many things that no child should witness, but I did. At one point it was a lot for me to handle. I would think about these experiences as a little girl, the things I went through, the things I saw that I could never unsee, and wondered what kind of world my own daughter would one day grow up in. If I had a daughter, what would she see? What would I show her? What kind of mother would I be for her?

What I've come to understand is that no family is perfect. No marriage is perfect. No parent-child relationship is perfect. No business team is perfect. Sometimes, we examine our lives through how we think other people live and wish our circumstances were different when they are exactly how they should be. All of our power is not in wishing but creating a different future by making different and better choices. I've come to understand that I am God's perfect creation. He sees my whole self. I only see a fraction of what he sees. I care that my daughter will be raised to understand this as well. And I want you to know that is true for you, too. This is for my daughter, but also for every little girl out there who needs to know what it takes…maybe this book can give them all some hope. If I can make it, so can you.

God Bless you,
Sabrina

8/16/2018
A Letter to my Unborn Daughter...

To My Dearest Daughter,

I want you to know that I thought a whole lot about you before you were even born.
I dreamed a life for you that I will never get to experience.
I prayed for your life and for you to be born when you were born.
I want you to always know how powerful you are.
I want you to always remember that you are sacred and special.
You are beautiful.
You were created in the image of something incredibly powerful.
That same power is inside of you and all around you.
Always remember that.
Never give your power away.
You will be a leader to the world.
Your life will be an example of greatness.
You will be admired for your strength, beauty, and grace.
Men and women around the world will honor you.
Your mother will always admire you and be grateful for the day that you were born.
You will live the life that I fought so hard to create for you.
I am already proud of what you will become.
I am grateful for the impact and light you will be to this world.
I thank God for your life.

With love,
Mom